Greece & Rome

NEW SURVEYS IN THE CLASSICS No. 36

ROMAN ORATORY

BY

CATHERINE STEEL

Published for the Classical Association

CAMBRIDGE UNIVERSITY PRESS

2006

Published by the Press Syndicate of the University of Cambridge
The Pitt Building, Trumpington Street, Cambridge, CB2 1RP
40 West 20th Street, New York, NY 10011-4211, USA
477 Williamstown Road, Port Melbourne, VIC 3207, Australia
Nautica Building, Beach Road, Cape Town 8005, South Africa

A catalogue record for this book is available from the British Library

ISBN 0 521 687225 (paperback)

Printed and bound by Bell and Bain, Glasgow, UK

CONTENTS

INTRODUCTION

The focus of this survey is on oratory as a spoken phenomenon, intimately related to politics and government at Rome. Its chronological scope is roughly from the beginning of the second century B.C. until the end of the first century A.D.; it has no pretensions to offer a guide to oratory in the later Empire. Its geographical focus is firmly on Rome, reflecting the overwhelming bias in our source material. I start with the occasions for oratory in Rome and turn then to the issues which arise from the process of turning a speech, delivered in front of an audience on a particular occasion, into a written text which can be accessed and enjoyed in private and at any time. I then consider some of the means by which orators of the imperial period explored different means of preserving their oratorical activities for posterity. In the final two chapters I concentrate on orators themselves: how they carried out their task, and reflected upon it, as adult practitioners, and then how boys became the next generation of orators.

The relatively narrow compass of the series has led to some omissions, even within the chronological limits outlined. There is less in the way of analysis of individual speeches than might be expected; texts have had to give way to performances. Moreover, this is not a book on Cicero; I have no intention of replacing A. E. Douglas' volume in this series.[1] And one consequence of shifting the focus from written to spoken is that Cicero is dislodged from the position of unquestioned pre-eminence he otherwise must hold. I have largely neglected the oratory of the second sophistic, even though its beginnings fall into the first century A.D.; this is with some regret, as the speeches in Greek which survive from the imperial period have as much claim to be considered as examples of 'Roman oratory' as do the two surviving examples in Latin from this period. But the overall environment in which these sophists were operating has its own set of codes and expectations, and I have been able to include only some brief glances at this area. But the previous volume in this series provides an excellent guide to recent work. Finally, I have made no attempt to consider the role of speeches within Roman historiography.

---

[1] Douglas (1968).

It remains only to thank those who have helped me with this project: Ian McAuslan, who commissioned the volume, and John Taylor, the editor of the series; Ewen Bowie, Alice Jenkins and Roger Rees for their helpful suggestions at various points in the process of writing; and Donal Bateson for his assistance with the image on the front cover.

Catherine Steel,
Glasgow, December 2005

I THE ORATOR IN ROMAN SOCIETY

Roman oratory consists of two distinct phenomena. One is the occasions when men – and, very seldom, women – spoke in public.[1] The other is the body of written texts of speeches which survive from antiquity. These are distinct objects of study: not all speeches were written down, not all those which were written down have survived; and even if we had all the speeches ever delivered, the written text can only convey a part of the experience of hearing an orator, in a particular place and time and with all the non-verbal aspects of rhetoric which contributed to an oratorical performance.[2] In this first chapter, I consider the various occasions on which individuals spoke at Rome, reserving until the second chapter the processes by which spoken performances were transferred into written texts.

The organisational structures of political life in Rome during the Republican period made oratory important in a variety of contexts. Political change depended, during most of this time, on the passage of legislation, and legislation in turn arose from meetings in which arguments were articulated orally in front of large groups of men before a vote was held. Political careers were based on success in elections for public office, and the capacity to present oneself effectively in speaking was one factor which might influence voting. And as the legal system permitted the vigorous scrutiny of the behaviour of magistrates, effective forensic oratory could be crucial to political survival. The three most important locations for civilian oratory were the *contio*, or public meeting, the Senate, and the law-courts: each imposed its own demands and constraints upon the orator. In addition, military commanders might expect to address both their troops and foreign powers; diplomatic oratory would also be required of envoys; and military and diplomatic activity were both normal occupations for the small group of elite males who also dominated domestic politics during the Republic.[3]

---

[1] Hortensia, the daughter of the great Republican orator Hortensius, spoke before the triumvirs in 42 B.C. against the financial demands they were making on married women (Quintilian, *Education of the Orator* 1.1.6; Appian, *Civil Wars* 4.32–34; Valerius Maximus 8.3.3). Valerius, however, knows only two other examples of female orators to use in his chapter on women who pleaded cases (8.3).

[2] On the possibilities of gesture see Aldrete (1999); Cairns (2005).

[3] On the range of tasks which a Roman in public life might find himself doing, see Beard and Crawford (1999: 55–59).

A *contio* was a gathering of the Roman citizen body.[4] It was not a voting assembly and, unlike voting assemblies, there did not need to be a considerable interval between the time when it was announced and the time when it was held. It therefore provided an opportunity to explain events to the people as they happened and to respond immediately to current crises. The auspices were not taken before it opened, and it is sometimes described as 'informal'. However, there were clear rules about its administration: a *contio* could only be summoned by a magistrate, and only those whom the summoner invited could address the crowd. The purpose of *contiones* was information and persuasion. One often followed immediately on the passing of senatorial decrees, at which the presiding magistrate would explain the Senate's decision to a waiting crowd;[5] and meetings were held frequently in the run up to legislative assemblies, in order to persuade the citizen body to support the proposal, culminating usually in one held just before the people voted. It seems, too, that the censors might address the people during the census.[6]

This variety of purposes within the *contio* led, unsurprisingly, to a variety of kinds of speech given at such meetings which reflects, in turn, the wide variation possible in a speaker's level of preparedness, motives in speaking and freedom to participate or not in the meeting. Many speeches at a *contio* would have been the result of considerable preparation and care, despite the seemingly *ad hoc* nature of such meetings, and the fact of their delivery could be known to the speaker weeks or months in advance. Into this category, above all, fall speeches in support of legislation, particularly where the legislation formed part of a magistrate's electoral campaign and when it was promulgated immediately upon entering into office. Much of the most notorious tribunician legislation of the late Republic must fall into this category, and would have been published as soon as tribunes entered office on 10 December. The proposer would thus have had a considerable period of time to prepare his campaign to secure his legislation's passage, should he be successful in gaining election. In

---

[4] On the *contio* see Pina Polo (1996); Laser (1997: 138–182); Millar (1998); Lintott (1999: 42–46); Mouritsen (2001); Morstein-Marx (2004).

[5] Cicero's *Second* and *Third Catilinarian* and *Fourth* and *Sixth Philippic* record his speeches at such *contiones*.

[6] No such speech survives complete; Cicero never held the censorship. But some fragments survive and these suggest that censors might use the opportunity to hammer home controversial moral messages. Quintus Metellus addressed the people on the subject of having more children in 131 B.C., and the emperor Augustus read out his speech to the Senate when proposing his family legislation (Malcovati 1976: frs. 4–7; Suetonius, *Life of Augustus* 89.2).

the interval between promulgation and voting, too, opponents would have time to prepare the case against, although opposition to contentious legislation frequently involved another tribune's veto or violent disruption as well as, or even instead of, oratory.[7]

A well-documented example of the passage of a law which involved extensive debate is that of the Manilian law in 66 B.C. This law proposed that Pompeius, who had just completed a strikingly fast and successful campaign against pirates in the Mediterranean, should be given extensive powers with which to fight Mithridates of Pontus. The passage of the law and the arguments used for and against it are unusually well documented, largely because Cicero delivered a speech in support of it which he then had disseminated in written form.[8]

Cicero's speech, *On the Command of Gnaeus Pompeius*, was the result of elaborate preparation. It marked the first occasion on which he addressed the people – as he indicates, at some length, at the beginning of the speech. Moreover, he need not have got involved in Manilius' campaign. He was just about to take office as praetor when the law was proposed, but there was no compulsion on magistrates to declare their opinions publicly about proposed legislation.[9] Indeed, Cicero's participation as a praetor is perhaps worth comment: Pina Polo identified only seven other praetors in the period from 133 B.C. to the end of the Republic who addressed *contiones*, and three of those held office in 44 B.C. – an exceptional year by any standards.[10] Cicero, therefore, went out of his way to take part in the campaign for this law, presumably by making an approach to Manilius once it became apparent that he was going to put forward this law and asking for the opportunity to speak at a *contio* that he would summon. Cicero's decision to do so may have been motivated in part by a belief that

---

[7] So, for example, opponents of Ti. Gracchus' agrarian law in 133 B.C. put up another tribune to veto the proposals and in 122 B.C. Livius Drusus' tactic in opposing Gaius Gracchus was to put forward an alternative legislative programme. The Gracchi were of course killed in office, as were Saturninus and the younger Livius Drusus (tr. pl. 91). Morstein-Marx (2004: 160–203) offers an excellent account of the presentation of opposing views in *contiones*.

[8] Steel (2001: 114–125)

[9] This timetable depends on Manilius' promulgating his law on or shortly after 10 December, with voting then possible from late December or early January, depending on when the market days fell. Tribunes of the people could request anyone's presence at a *contio*, and there are occasions when a tribune might bring an opponent to a public meeting; but there are very few occasions where someone who was not taking a stand on an issue was nonetheless brought forward in this way.

[10] Pina Polo (1996: 189). The others are M. Marius Gratidianus (85); C. Julius Caesar (62); Ap. Claudius (57); and M. Porcius Cato (54). Some occasions may well not be attested in surviving sources, but nonetheless these figures suggest that it was distinctly unusual for a praetor to address the people, even after Sulla's reforms which meant that they were regularly in Rome during their term of office.

Pompeius was indeed needed to fight Mithridates, or it may not; but it was undoubtedly a decision which could have benefits for his own career. Pompeius was very popular with the Roman people at this point, and supporting him offered Cicero – whose eyes were firmly fixed on the election for the consulship of 63, which would be held in the summer of 64, little more than two years' distant – a chance to create a link with the great man which would benefit him in those elections.[11] Cicero's involvement is the result of very careful reflection and planning.

This care and planning are reflected in the written version, and there is no reason to believe that it marks a substantial rewriting of the oral version.[12] The bulk of the speech consists of an encomium of Pompeius' virtues, carefully constructed to emphasise his value to the Roman state.[13] But towards the end of the speech Cicero responds directly to criticisms of Manilius' law which had been made in speeches by Hortensius and Quintus Catulus.[14] Both these men had held the consulship, and Hortensius was one of the most distinguished orators of the day. Their speeches do not survive, and indeed there is no evidence that either disseminated a written version of what they had said. But some record of what they said, independent of Cicero's representation, is likely to have survived, because Plutarch preserves an anecdote about Catulus' speech: 'Catulus . . . ordered the Senate . . . repeatedly to find some hill or crag, like their ancestors, to which it could flee and preserve its freedom'.[15] Cicero's response to Hortensius and Catulus is likely to include some tendentious misrepresentation of the arguments, and it is not easy to distinguish in his speech between the arguments Hortensius and Catulus used to oppose the Gabinian law the previous year (which gave Pompeius an extraordinary command against the pirates) and those employed against the Manilian law. Morstein-Marx suggests that they may have spoken in 66 at a *contio* summoned by Manilius at which he gave his opponents the opportunity to speak in order to demonstrate both to them and, more importantly, to the Roman

---

[11] Mitchell (1979: 153–165).

[12] See further Chapter 2 below.

[13] Steel (2001: 130–156).

[14] Cicero, *On the Command of Gnaeus Pompeius* 51–68.

[15] Plutarch, *Life of Pompey* 30.4, Κάτλος . . . ἐκέλευε τὴν βουλὴν . . . πολλάκις ὄρος ζητεῖν ὥσπερ οἱ πρόγονοι καὶ κρημνόν, ὅπου καταφυγοῦσα διασώσει τὴν ἐλευθερίαν. This fragment sounds very plausible because of its paradoxical use of the idea of the secession of the plebs (Morstein-Marx 2004: 183). Sallust's *Histories* may have continued into 66, in which case it is possible he included versions of Catulus' and Hortensius' speeches; a version of Catulus' speech opposing the Gabinian law appears to survive in the fragments of book 5.

people, that opposition to his proposal was futile.[16] Certainly, neither Hortensius nor Catulus held a magistracy in 66 B.C. and there is no record of any of the tribunes of 66 opposing Manilius' law, so it is not clear who else might have provided them with the opportunity of addressing the people by summoning a *contio*. Nonetheless, even if they were restricted in time and facing a hostile audience, both would have had advance notice of the law and thus the opportunity to formulate arguments with which to oppose it.

Cicero's account of the arguments used by the opponents of the Manilian law may not be strictly accurate but the amount of his own speech which he devotes to them is nonetheless suggestive. The appearance of debate was important. There may have been no doubt that this law would be passed: but it seems that it was rhetorically effective to be heard to counter the opposition's points. Doing so also generated a result of particular interest to Cicero himself: it demonstrated his respect for these two senior figures and thus is a crucial element in the care which *On the Command* as a whole manifests in not alienating the more conservative element within the Senate.

Another example of carefully prepared contional oratory is the speech of thanks Cicero delivered to the people on his return from exile in 57 B.C. This speech, and its companion one delivered immediately beforehand to the Senate, marked his re-entry into Roman public life. He had had plenty of time to consider how best to do this: confident that the law recalling him would be passed, he left Dyrrachium on 4 August, reaching Brundisium the following day. His journey up through Italy took a further month and he entered Rome on 4 September, giving the two public speeches of thanks the following day.[17] The occasion was absolutely crucial to Cicero's continued public career: he needed to consolidate the current of opinion which had allowed the passage of the law recalling him, in order to reintegrate himself into Roman public life and demonstrate that his exile, and the political weaknesses which had led up to it, were now firmly in the past. Saying exactly the right things was extremely important. In fact, the speech in the Senate is the only one which we know Cicero gave with the assistance of written notes, in order that he did not forget to thank any particular individual.[18] Both speeches are short, but each is effectively tailored to its audience and

---

[16] Morstein-Marx (2004: 179–186).
[17] Marinone (2004: 110–111).
[18] Cicero, *On Behalf of Plancius* 74

attempts to place Cicero back into the community which he is addressing.[19]

However, there were aspects of the delivery of *Thanks to the People on his Return* which Cicero could not be sure of in advance, and these are part of a wider set of uncertainties relating to his return from exile as a whole. He could not be sure of the audience which would greet him as he returned, in terms either of size or of attitude. In a letter to Atticus written shortly afterwards he emphasises mass rejoicing:

Whilst at Brundisium . . . I gathered, from a letter from my brother Quintus, that the law had been passed by the *comitia centuriata* accompanied by enormous enthusiasm on the part of all classes and ages and with an enormous gathering from all over Italy. I was treated with great pomp by the Brundisians and as I travelled envoys came from all over to congratulate me. My entry into the city was such that no-one whose name is known to a *nomenclator* failed to meet me, except those of my enemies who could not pretend or deny their enmity.[20]

But even with Quintus' encouraging news Cicero could not be completely sure of his welcome: he could not have known for certain how effective his friends and supporters would have been in generating mass enthusiasm and crowds when he entered the city, nor how many might wish to stay and listen to him, and how many supporters of his enemy Clodius might be making their feelings known. To that extent, at least, he would have had to have remained flexible in preparing what he might say to a greater extent than when contributing to the debate on the Manilian law. Indeed, the entire situation was fairly novel. Legislative *contiones* were frequent events: a politician would know, in general terms, what was expected when he spoke. But very few politicians returned from exile. The most recent example, before Cicero, was Metellus Numidicus, who was exiled in 100 and returned in 99. There was no fixed template for what might happen in these circumstances, and whilst in theory this allowed Cicero great freedom to present himself as he wished he also had no conventions to rely on. The contional oratory of his return from exile combined elaborate preparation with a considerable degree of uncertainty.

At the *contiones* so far considered, orators gave speeches which they had prepared. Other *contiones* were very carefully stage-managed, but

---

[19] Mack (1937); Nicholson (1992).

[20] Cicero, *Letters to Atticus* 4.1.4–5, *cognoui, cum Brundisi essem, litteris Quinti fratris mirifico studio omnium aetatum atque ordinum, incredibili concursu Italiae, legem comitiis centuriatis esse perlatam. inde a Brundisinis honestissime ornatus iter ita feci ut undique ad me cum gratulatione legati conuenerint. ad urbem ita ueni ut nemo ullius ordinis homo nomenclatori notus fuerit qui mihi obuiam non uenerit, praeter eos inimicos quibus id ipsum, se inimicos esse, non liceret aut dissimulare aut negare.*

the essential information was conveyed by witnesses who were themselves not the central political figures. In the aftermath of the death of Clodius in 52 B.C., one of his supporters, T. Munatius Plancus, 'brought forward in a public meeting M. Aemilius Philemon, a well-known man and freedman of M. Lepidus, who said that he along with four free men had happened to be passing while Clodius was being killed, and when they cried out at it were seized and taken to Milo's villa, where they were kept shut up for two months'.[21] Munatius Plancus would not have taken any chances on what Philemon would say: Philemon may have been telling the truth, but Plancus will have briefed him carefully on what to say. Comparable is the appearance of Vettius at a *contio* in 59. This man, whom Cicero describes as a well-known informer, testified in the Senate about an alleged plot to assassinate Pompeius.[22] Immediately after this meeting of the Senate its decree was read out to a *contio*; the following day Caesar, one of the consuls, called a *contio* at which he gave Vettius the opportunity to speak. According to Cicero, Vettius 'said everything about the state which he wished to; he was thoroughly prepared for the task'.[23] Cicero's letter also suggests that Vettius gave a full-scale speech, rather than simply answering questions put to him by the presiding magistrate, which was probably the case at the *contio* at which Philemon gave his evidence.[24] Certainly Cicero's description of the meeting indicates his own sense of the impropriety of Vettius' getting such an opportunity to speak, since he compares him first to the senior consular Catulus, whom Caesar forced to speak at a meeting from the ground rather than the platform, and then to Bibulus, Caesar's colleague as consul during 59 who was at this point confined to his house in fear of violence.

Another point of interest about this *contio* is that everything seems not to have gone to plan, despite the careful preparation. After the meeting had been dismissed the tribune Vatinius summoned it back for Vettius to make one last observation, implicating two more men in the plot against Pompeius. This manoeuvre suggests either that

---

[21] Asc. 38C, *T. Munatius Plancus tribunus plebis produxerat in contionem M. Aemilium Philemonem, notum hominem, libertum M. Lepidi, qui se dicebat pariterque secum quattuor liberos homines iter facientes superuenisse, cum Clodius occideretur, et ob id cum proclamassent, abreptos et perductos in uillam Milonis per duos mensis praeclusos fuisse.*

[22] Cicero, *Letters to Atticus* 2.24.2–4; Taylor (1950).

[23] Cicero, *Letters to Atticus* 2.24.3, *hic ille omnia quae uoluit de re publica dixit, ut qui illuc factus institutusque uenisset.*

[24] Question and answer seems to have been the usual method when private individuals were introduced at public meetings, insofar as one can generalise from a very small number of attested cases: cf. Valerius Maximus 3.8.6.

Vettius had been briefed to include them, and forgot, or that it had belatedly occurred to Caesar, or Vatinius, that it would be advantageous to include them. Even carefully orchestrated public meetings might not run entirely according to plan.

There were also occasions when a politician had to be able to address the people on the spur of the moment. Speaking to the people after a senatorial debate falls into this category, inasmuch as the outcome of a debate could not be known with certainty in advance. But the oratorical challenge of this kind of speech need not have been great if the presiding magistrate was simply providing information: indeed, little more may have been needed than that the senatorial resolution be read aloud. More impromptu, and more demanding, were occasions when popular feelings needed immediate assuaging. Cicero's career provides two particularly striking instances where he spoke at a *contio* without preparation. Towards the end of 66 B.C., when Cicero was praetor in charge of the extortion court, Manilius – who had on 9 December come to the end of his period as tribune of the people – was charged in front of this court.[25] Cicero apparently resisted Manilius' attempt to have his trial postponed, granting him only one day's adjournment; the people protested, and the tribunes summoned Cicero to a hastily gathered *contio* where they questioned him as to his actions. He defended himself by claiming that he had wished to ensure that Manilius faced trial with a sympathetic praetor, that is himself, in charge of the court. This mollified the people, who then demanded that he defend Manilius when he did come to trial; and Cicero agreed to do this. Although the eventual outcome seems not to have been harmful to Cicero – Quintus Cicero refers to this episode as one of those which built Cicero's reputation and popularity – it is implausible to imagine that he had set up the whole sequence of events in advance. Rather, this is an instance of Cicero fumbling, however briefly, in his attempt to maintain his universal appeal; and being forced to resort to his oratorical skills to attempt to retrieve the situation.

The second example is from 63 B.C., when Cicero was consul. At a theatrical performance during the year, Roscius Otho was hissed by the crowd; the cause of their hostility was the fact that when Otho had been tribune in 67 B.C. he had proposed a law which re-established privileged seating in the theatre for the equestrian class.[26] Cicero

---

[25] Plutarch, *Life of Cicero* 9.4–7; Dio 36.44; Quintus Cicero, *Notes on Electioneering* 51; Ramsay (1980); J. Crawford (1984: 64–69, 1994: 33–41).

[26] J. Crawford (1994: 209–214).

interrupted the festival, called an impromptu meeting in front of the temple of Bellona, and spoke with such force that the people returned to the theatre and applauded Roscius. It is possible that Cicero had picked up some advance warning that a disturbance might take place, and hence had a chance at least to reflect upon the sorts of arguments he might wish to use; but that is supposition, and even if he was not taken entirely unawares, the circumstances were unpredictable and rapidly developing. Cicero's securing an outcome he would regard as successful was largely due to his capacity to speak to the people in an impromptu setting. It is worth noting that he chose to have a version of what he had said disseminated.[27]

Cicero's surviving speeches at *contiones* apart from the Manilian law speech are rather different from these impromptu situations. They were all delivered after senatorial meetings and as summaries of those debates for the benefit of the waiting people: there is reasonable evidence that a crowd would gather outside the Senate house towards the end of contentious debates in order to hear the outcome as soon as possible. The speaker's job on such occasions was primarily to provide an accurate summary. Indeed, the person delivering such a speech would not necessarily be someone who regularly addressed the people: the task was likely to devolve upon the magistrate who had presided over the session of the Senate, or one of his senior colleagues. It is interesting to note that there are relatively few examples of this kind of speech being disseminated in written form, which would suggest that it was not regarded as offering a particular good showcase for oratorical talent.

There is one more type of oratory in front of the people to be considered: funeral oratory.[28] The funerals of members of famous families at Rome were public events, with a procession to the Rostra where a speech was delivered in praise of the deceased; the procession included men impersonating office-holders from earlier generations of the family, wearing the robes of the highest position they had obtained, and the speech included a rehearsal of the deeds of these men.[29] It is unclear whether or not these gatherings were formally *contiones* or not, nor is the mechanism whereby someone was deemed eligible for a funeral of this sort absolutely transparent. Nonetheless, this was another category of oratory where the audience was the

[27] Cicero, *Letters to Atticus* 2.1.3; one fragment of the speech survives.
[28] Kierdorf (1980); Flower (1996: 128–158).
[29] Polybius 6.53–54.

citizen body as a whole.[30] The speaker seems to have been the eldest son, where that was possible; and a written version of the speech was often disseminated.

The second major forum for oratory in the Republic was the Senate, whose deliberations were structured around the exchange of oral opinions. Although the Senate's decisions were never, during the Republic, legally binding in formal terms they had the force of law if they were not vetoed; and matters of urgent importance to the *res publica*, particularly though not exclusively in the field of foreign affairs, were regularly decided by this body. The format of debates appears to have followed a clear set of conventions: the presiding magistrate stated the proposal, and may have indicated his opinion on it; he then asked the opinion of those present, starting with the most senior figures.[31] The order in which men were asked to contribute was fixed at the first meeting of the year, when the newly elected consul who held the *fasces* in January conducted his first meeting.[32] As the presiding officer moved through his list, the responses seem to have become briefer and briefer as the speakers merely indicated their agreement with one or other of the positions previously articulated. Nonetheless, it seems that all senators present had to be asked their opinion before the matter could be put to the vote. As meetings had to be concluded by nightfall this opened up the possibility of filibustering; and even when filibustering was not the aim, a senator was free to raise matters outside the scope of the proposal which was formally under discussion.[33] One peculiarity of the Republican Senate was that it did not have a single location for its meetings: although there was a Senate House, at the edge of the Forum, the Senate itself could meet in any consecrated space.[34] Its first meeting of the year was, by tradition, held in the temple of Jupiter on the Capitoline; it could meet outside the city boundaries when it wished to allow an

---

[30] Polybius, whose detailed description is surely based on being present at such a funeral himself, treats such funerals as devices to inspire courage and emulation among its men: 'the most important result is that young men are inspired to endure extremes on behalf of the common good in order to win the glory which accompanies brave men' (τὸ δὲ μέγιστον, οἱ νέοι παρορμῶνται πρὸς τὸ πᾶν ὑπομένειν ὑπὲρ τῶν κοινῶν πραγμάτων χάριν τοῦ τύχειν τῆς συνακολουθούσης τοῖς ἀγαθοῖς τῶν ἀνδρῶν εὐκλείας. I discuss the delivery of funeral speeches in more detail in Chapter 2.

[31] Lintott (1999: 77–78).

[32] See, for example, Cicero, *Letters to Atticus* 1.13.2, in which Cicero gives the order in which the consul Piso asked the first four consulars in 61 B.C.

[33] Lintott (1999: 78).

[34] Bonnefond-Coudry (1989: 25–160).

imperium-holder to attend; and a number of other temples were used on occasion for meetings. The choice of location lay with the presiding consul; in 63 B.C. Cicero seems to have chosen the temple of Jupiter Stator with particular care to be the place where he revealed Catilina's designs to the Senate, since it enabled him to appeal for protection for the state to a deity associated with a successful counter-attack during a battle.[35]

This highly formalised structure of debate would thus seem to offer to all members of the Senate the opportunity to speak on a regular basis. However, in practice it was extremely unusually for junior senators to offer substantial contributions. Indeed, those senators who had held only the quaestorship – and in the post-Sullan Senate they formed the vast majority – were nicknamed *pedarii*, those who voted with their feet. Very few substantial speeches are recorded as having being delivered to the Senate by men who had not reached the praetorship.[36]

The debate on the fate of the Catilinarian conspirators in December 63 B.C. is an exception worth consideration. This meeting of the Senate was notable not only for the gravity of the subject; important contributions were also made by the relatively junior.[37] Julius Caesar – then praetor-elect – argued for life imprisonment for the conspirators, after Cicero had opened the debate and Dec. Junius Silanus, one of the consuls-elect, had spoken strongly in favour of the death penalty. Everyone who had spoken before Caesar had supported Silanus' proposal, a group which included fourteen ex-consuls.[38] After Caesar spoke, opinion was apparently divided between the two proposals until the younger Cato restated the case for execution and proposed a new motion, including praise of Cicero. It was Cato's proposal which was the one eventually passed. Cato was at that point only a tribune-elect, having held the quaestorship the previous year; yet his speech is presented as crucial in bringing the Senate back to support of the death penalty.[39]

The way in which Cato's contribution to this debate was perceived seems to have been affected by his subsequent career: Cicero complains, on reading Brutus' life of Cato in 45 B.C., that he has misunderstood the course of the debate because he seems not to

---

[35] Cicero, *First Catilinarian*; Vasaly (1993: 49–59).
[36] Bonnefond-Coudry (1989: 655–682).
[37] Sallust's *Conspiracy of Catiline* 50–53 offers versions of both speeches; on the complexity of the debate, not reflected in Sallust, see Drummond (1995: 23–77).
[38] Cicero, *Letters to Atticus* 12.21.1.
[39] Sallust, *Catiline* 53.1; Dio 37.36.3.

know that all the consulars, who spoke much earlier, supported the death penalty.[40] Sallust's account is structured to pit Caesar against Cato, foreshadowing future events and neglecting other speakers. But even allowing for subsequent distortions, it is clear that the course of this particular debate was not firmly fixed by the initial speakers. The contributions of Caesar and, even more, Cato, demonstrate that a more junior man of vigour and courage could contribute to senatorial debate, even if, most of the time, convention and the norms of orderly debate privileged the senior. But one should be slightly wary of under-estimating Cato's position at this time: he had already joined the minority of senators who would hold office beyond the quaestorship as well as beginning the creation of his reputation as a public servant of formidable, and even repulsive, integrity; and he had a distin-guished family history to appeal to.[41] He was not, even in 63, a humble foot-soldier.

The evidence on the speeches of Cato and Caesar suggest that they were carefully crafted pieces of oratory. And evidence from Cicero's letters shows that he too regarded the Senate as an appropriate audi-ence for oratorical fireworks. Early in 61 B.C., soon after Pompeius returned to Rome, there was a meeting of the Senate at which the presiding consul asked Pompeius what his views were on the Senate's response to alleged sacrilege at the Bona Dea ceremony the previous December.[42] Pompeius' reply was brief, but when Crassus' turn came he apparently gave an elaborate speech praising Cicero for the very continuation of his civic existence; and later in the same debate Cicero too gave a polished speech about the contemporary situation, which he describes with a string of Greek rhetorical terms. Many contributions to senatorial debate may have been brief and unelaborate, but orators could display the full range of their talents.

The third major occasion for oratory in the Republic was offered by the law-courts.[43] Ultimate judicial authority in criminal cases lay with the Roman people, but increasingly during the Republic this authority was delegated to juries who tried cases under a variety of statutes. The administration of civil law was the responsibility of the *praetor urbanus*. Both types of case involved advocacy.

Civil law was the subject of intense intellectual effort in the last decades of the Republic and a distinct category of legal experts

---

[40] Cicero, *Letters to Atticus* 12.21.1.
[41] On Cato's conduct as quaestor, see Plutarch, *Life of the Younger Cato* 16–18.
[42] Cicero, *Letters to Atticus* 1.14.2–4.
[43] Fantham (2004: 102–130); Lintott (2005).

arose.[44] Civil cases provided opportunities for oratory, despite the much smaller audience than in criminal cases, and could attract very distinguished advocates. One case at least achieved enduring notoriety: the so-called *causa Curiana*, which pitted L. Licinius Crassus against Q. Mucius Scaevola in the centumviral court (which dealt with inheritance).[45] Cicero discusses this case at length in both *On the Orator* and *Brutus*, and quotes some of Crassus' speech in the former, strongly suggesting that Crassus did disseminate a written version.[46] Cicero himself was active in civil cases and published a number of them.[47] Interestingly, however, the latest written version is from 69 B.C., which suggests that once he had established a reputation as an orator and was being asked to appear in criminal cases it was no longer necessary to spend time in disseminating civil cases.[48]

The oratorical opportunities provided by criminal law were more exciting.[49] The audience was bigger: there was a large jury as well as interested bystanders. The facts were more enticing: not dry legal discussion but murder, assault and treason. And the political implications were often considerable. Roman criminal law, particularly in the period after Sulla's reorganisation of the courts, was concerned primarily with threats to the state.[50] As well, therefore, as murder and assault, treason, electoral bribery and provincial extortion were all covered by standing courts. The last three were by definition political crimes, and in the increasingly violent atmosphere of the 60s and 50s the law on violence was used against the politically active. The legal system was, indeed, one of the most effective ways of controlling senior magistrates in the exercise of their *imperium* as the penalties (capital, but always at this period avoidable by exile) put an end permanently to the guilty individual's political activity.

There was no public prosecution service: criminal charges were brought by individuals. Engaging in a prosecution seems to have been something which required careful consideration: given that the

---

[44] Frier (1985); Harries (2004).

[45] Scaevola argued for a strict interpretation in accordance with the exact words of Curius' will; Crassus successfully argued for the intention of the will to be honoured. See Cicero, *On the Orator* 1.180–182; *Brutus* 194–198; Fantham (2004: 117–121).

[46] Strongly, but not conclusively; Cicero was very likely present at this trial, given his family's contacts with Crassus (Rawson 1971) and may have made notes at the time.

[47] Of these, *On Behalf of Publius Quinctius*, *On Behalf of Quintus Roscius the Actor*, and *On Behalf of Aulus Caecina* survive largely intact and *On Behalf of Tullius* in a much more fragmentary state.

[48] See further below, Chapter 2.

[49] See Tacitus, *Dialogus* 20 on the limited attractions of reading civil cases.

[50] Riggsby (1999).

penalties were so severe, the habitual prosecutor could gain a reputation for cruelty and this impression was strengthened by the benefits
which a successful prosecution conferred on the prosecutor.[51]
Furthermore, an unsuccessful prosecution often led to lasting hostility
between prosecutor and accused. Some people did occupy themselves
regularly with prosecution, but among those engaged in or aspiring
towards an office-holding career prosecution was engaged in, if at all,
only once and at the start of one's career.[52] Cicero's prosecution of
Verres in 70 B.C. might seem to fit into this category, but some caution
is required. He had made his debut as an orator ten years earlier, and
by 70 was not a novice but a man of thirty-six seeking election to the
aedileship. It is possible that his decision to engage in a prosecution
was motivated by the slow development of his forensic practice as a
defender and the consequent lack of opportunities to display his
talents as a speaker.[53] And he is very careful to present his prosecution of Verres as though it were a defence of his Sicilian and Roman
victims. Prosecution was not something which senior politicians
undertook regularly.

Acting for the defence carried with it none of the potential stigma
of prosecution. 'It is defending, above all, which creates glory and
gratitude, and all the more so when the person defended seems to be
harassed and threatened by the resources of a powerful man.'[54] The
problem with defence, however, was that the orator had to be asked.
That meant having already acquired a reputation. Starting one's
public career with a prosecution was thus a way of breaking this
vicious circle.

Despite these links between politics and criminal prosecution, by
no means all of Cicero's activity as a criminal advocate had political
significance. His practice varied over time: perhaps unsurprisingly, as
he became better known as an advocate and more prominent himself
politically, his forensic practice came more and more to include the
defence of prominent politicians.

Thus far I have considered oratory at Rome during the Republic.
Roman officials had occasion to speak outside Rome as well. In
rhetorical terms, this kind of oratory is deliberative: but the

---

[51] Cicero, *On Duties* 2.49–51 discusses the circumstances in which prosecution is acceptable.

[52] See Tacitus, *Dialogus* 34.7, though Tacitus appears to underestimate the ages of some of
those involved: see Mayer (2001) *ad loc*. On prosecutors, see further Chapter 3.

[53] Steel (2005: 25).

[54] Cicero, *On Duties* 2.51, *maxime autem et gloria paritur et gratia defensionibus, eoque maior si
quando accidit ut ei subueniatur qui potentis alicuius opibus circumueniri urgerique uideatur.*

circumstances of performance in terms of audience and aims make these occasions distinctly different from speeches within the Senate. Moreover, the concern within Roman culture with the concept of a just war and the need to establish that Roman wars were justified led to the development of exemplary narratives in which the oral communication of Rome's policy is crucial.[55]

An example is the meeting between the Illyrian queen Teuta and two Roman envoys in 230 B.C. Illyrian pirates had been attacking Italian shipping; the Italians complained to Rome, and the Senate sent envoys to ask the Illyrian ruler to desist. In Polybius' account, the ruler was a woman, Teuta; and at the meeting between her and the envoys, the two Romans made their complaint and Teuta replied that, whilst the Illyrian state did not have hostile intentions towards Rome, the private actions of individual Illyrian sailors was not something with which the rulers of Illyria had traditionally interfered.[56] There follows the reply of the younger of the envoys: 'The Romans, Teuta, have a very fine custom of punishing wrongs committed privately by public action and of helping those who have been injured. We shall endeavour, with God's help, vigorously and swiftly to compel you to correct your royal behaviour towards the Illyrians.'[57] And Teuta was so enraged by this reply that she arranged for the envoys to be assassinated, thus precipitating the first Illyrian war. Polybius' account is very clearly drawn from a pro-Roman source – perhaps that of Fabius Pictor – which sought to justify Roman behaviour by positing insult and then assassination.[58] The envoy's actual words must be conjectural and indeed the meeting itself may well never have happened. But its importance in the subsequent historical tradition shows that what was said during diplomatic exchanges was regarded as important; and so, in turn, the Romans who were likely to find themselves in such a situation had good reason to value the skills which would make them effective diplomatic orators.

The Illyrian episode shows us a Roman envoy responding in an impromptu fashion to what must be understood as an insult, without consideration for how his words will be received. Indeed, this is

---

[55] On the concept of the just war, see Albert (1980); Ramage (2001: 145–148).

[56] Polybius 2.8.6–13; Appian's account (*Illyrian War* 7) has no record of any meeting between the envoys and Illyrians, as they are killed before they can land.

[57] Polybius 2.8.10–11, 'Ρωμαίοις μέν, ὦ Τεύτα, κάλλιστον ἔθος ἐστὶ τὰ κατ' ἰδίαν ἀδικήματα κοινῇ μεταπορεύεσθαι καὶ βοηθεῖν τοῖς ἀδικουμένοις· πειρασόμεθα δὴ θεοῦ βουλομένου σφόδρα καὶ ταχέως ἀναγκάσαι σε τὰ βασιλικὰ νόμιμα διορθώσασθαι πρός Ἰλλυριούς.

[58] Walbank (1957: 153, 158–160).

central to how Polybius – and presumably his source – set up the story: a young man, responding without premeditation to provocation and thereby showing the virtue of Rome compared to untrustworthy foreigners.[59] Other episodes – and ones which are based on rather more secure evidence – indicate Romans fully conscious of the opportunities which speech abroad gave them both to promote Rome, and their own reputations. Two examples which took place relatively early in Rome's encounter with the Greek world show these possibilities and also suggest that divergent views on how best to speak as a Roman abroad were current from the outset of Rome's history as a Mediterranean power.

In 196 B.C. Ti. Quinctius Flamininus, the Roman commander in Greece, recently successful over the armies of Philip V of Macedon, made an announcement to the crowds gathered to celebrate the Isthmian games. His audience were anxious. The Romans' military victories had established them now as the dominant force in mainland Greece; the question was what sort of rulers they would prove to be. In particular, there was doubt over the status of a number of cities of crucial strategic value, including Corinth. If the Romans kept garrisons in these cities, then the statements that the Roman commission, which had been sent out to establish the new form of government, had made indicating that the Greeks would be free to use their own laws would be largely undermined. Flamininus had a herald read out a proclamation which provided the answer in a single sentence: 'The Senate of Rome and Titus Quinctius Flamininus the pro-consul, having defeated king Philip and the Macedonians in war, leave free, ungarrisoned, untaxed and able to use their ancestral laws Corinth; Phocis; Locri; Euboea; Phthiotic Achaea; Magnesia; Thessaly; and Perrhaebia.'[60]

Flamininus' address conveyed to his audience reassurance and a promise of independence from Roman interference: attractive messages, of which the Greeks were in practice to be disappointed. But, setting aside the question of Flamininus' sincerity, his desire to be seen as a philhellene is unmistakable. Other Romans took steps to project a different character. Five years after the Isthmian pronouncement, the elder Cato found himself in Athens as a military tribune in

---

[59] It is the younger envoy who speaks; and what he says is 'fitting, but not opportune'. An extra frisson is added to the narrative by Teuta's gender.
[60] Polybius 18.46.5, "Ἡ σύγκλητος ἡ Ῥωμαίων καὶ Τίτος Κοΐντιος στρατηγὸς ὕπατος, καταπολεμήσαντες βασιλέα Φίλιππον καὶ Μαχεδόνας, ἀφιᾶσιν ἐλευθέρους, ἀφρουρήτους, ἀφορολογήτους, νόμοις χρωμένους τοῖς πατρίοις, Κορινθίους, Φωκέας, Λοκρούς, Εὐβοεῖς, Ἀχαιοὺς τοὺς Φθίωτας, Μάγνητας, Θετταλούς, Περραιβούς.'

the aftermath of the Roman defeat of Antiochus. According to Plutarch, whose ultimate source must here be Cato himself, he addressed the Athenian assembly in Latin, and then his words were translated. The interpreter spoke at much greater length than Cato had done, leading to admiration among the Athenian audience, and allowing Cato to conclude that 'Greeks speak with their lips, but Romans from the heart'.[61] The episode set up a contrast between wordy, insincere Greeks and laconic, honest Romans, with the added suggestion that the two languages themselves contributed to these characteristics. And as Gruen points out, the incident, if it did indeed take place, could only have done so as a result of Cato's consciously stage-managing the scene: his interpreter would only have inflated his translation if Cato had instructed him so to do.[62] Cato was attempting to reinforce the superiority of Rome through the nature of his oratorical performance as well as the content of his speech. And although the initial audience was the gathered Athenians, the telling of the episode in the *Origines* was surely intended to reassure Romans both of Cato's integrity as a Roman speaker, even when operating far from Rome, and of the capacity of the Latin language itself to withstand the pressures of overseas rule. Latin is indeed the proper language of empire.[63]

Neither Flamininus nor Cato spoke in Greek. Later, some Roman officials did. The evidence for such occasions suggests that some Romans were conscious of benefits in being seen to be fluent, during the conduct of official business, in Greek. Crassus Mucianus, when proconsul in Asia Minor in 131 B.C., was able to conduct judicial business in five separate dialects of Greek, taking his cue from the language spoken by the plaintiff.[64] The central point of the anecdote, for Quintilian and Valerius Maximus, is Mucianus' intellectual capacity; but the story also shows us a Roman official demonstrating his authority through knowing Greek better than the Greeks themselves. Over fifty years later Cicero addressed the Syracusan senate in Greek during the course of his evidence-gathering against Verres; we know this because Cicero tells his audience so in the fourth *Verrine*, ostensibly in response to criticism from L. Caecilius Metellus, Verres' successor as governor of Sicily, that it was not in keeping with the

---

[61] Plutarch, *Cato the Elder* 12.5, τὰ ῥήματα τοῖς μὲν Ἕλλησιν ἀπὸ χειλέων, τοῖς δὲ Ῥωμαίοις ἀπὸ καρδίας φέρεσθαι.

[62] Gruen (1992: 64–65).

[63] On the Romans' construction of Latin as morally superior to Greek, see Farrell (2001: 30–32).

[64] Quintilian, *Education of the Orator* 11.2.50; cf. Valerius Maximus 8.7.6.

dignity of a Roman official to use Greek.[65] In the *Verrines* this anecdote is part of a sustained comparison of Cicero and Verres in which
Verres' ignorance of Greek culture is paraded as a cause for shame.
From the perspective, however, of Roman diplomatic oratory, it can
be used as an example of one Roman's sensitivity to the value of
speaking in relation to securing local good-will, and to the added
effectiveness which could arise from speaking to the audience in their
own language.[66]

Oratory was a matter of crucial importance in the political life of
Rome, and a highly useful skill for any politician. So much, at least,
can be accepted without difficulty for the Republican period, where
popular election, the potential for vigorous legal scrutiny of public
behaviour and senatorial government combined to make addressing
an audience effectively a significant activity, be that audience citizens,
jurors or senators. The situation from the principate of Augustus
onwards was rather different: many decisions were made behind
closed doors among small groups whose deliberations were not
recorded, and from the reign of Tiberius onwards the capacity to elect
magistrates was removed from the citizen body and given to the
Senate.[67] From this point onwards, the emperor had a decisive role in
controlling entry to the Senate. It is reasonable, therefore, to expect
that the orator's position in Roman society should change as oratory
itself took on different roles.

One of the curious aspects, however, of oratory at Rome is how
much continuity there is in the functions of oratory between Republic
and Empire. Public meetings, it is true, largely cease to be relevant to
the tasks of the orator from the reign of Augustus onwards.[68] But the
Senate and the law-courts remain locations for skilled public speaking
and the capacity to speak well remains a valuable asset for a politician.
Moreover, in formal terms the mechanics of senatorial debate remain
remarkably unchanged.[69] The presiding officer determined which
items were for discussion, and debate proceeded by his calling
members present in order of seniority. In theory, then, even junior
senators would have an opportunity to speak and there is a reasonable
amount of evidence to suggest that on occasion some of them did.
However, the practicalities of getting through business suggest that

[65] Cicero, *Verrines* 4.147.
[66] As Adams points out (2003: 9–14) such anecdotes are of little use in determining bilingualism.
[67] Tacitus, *Annals* 1.15.
[68] Mayer (2001: 193).
[69] Talbert (1984: 221–289).

debates could be brought to a close before all had contributed, particularly if they were not controversial; and presumably many senators will have given their opinion simply by indicating that they agreed with an earlier speaker.

Nonetheless, the dynamics of these locations for speaking are changed utterly by the presence, or potential presence, of the emperor.[70] The Senate House becomes one of the chief locations for the emperor to articulate the nature of his rule: how he handles the Senate and the debates in it are now a major index of the kind of emperor he wishes to be.[71] Moreover, it is a truism of imperial history that decision-making is transferred from public areas to private ones: emperors made decisions in consultation with close advisers, who were not necessarily themselves members of the senatorial elite.[72] Oratory's relationship with power and authority becomes oblique.

Against this background of severely restricted freedom as a deliberative body, the Senate did, in fact, expand the scope of its activities during the first century A.D. to include forensic matters on a regular basis.[73] In particular, it judged cases where the defendant was a member of the Senate, so repetundae and maiestas cases came increasingly under its jurisdiction; and it could judge other cases where the defendant was a senator. It also intervened in matters where there were serious implications for the state as a whole: an example of such a case is the collapse of an amphitheatre at Fidenae in A.D. 27. The Senate not only exiled the builder responsible, but also drafted regulations concerning the construction of such buildings to apply thereafter across the Empire.[74] This expansion of the Senate's scope into forensic matters brought with it many more opportunities for senators to speak, and indeed, on occasion, obligations to do so. Both prosecutors and defenders could be assigned by the Senate, by choice or through the lot, and those chosen could not refuse the job unless they had been exempted.[75] Thus the change in senatorial function in the imperial period brought with it a new obligation on senators to be competent speakers. By no means all senators in the Republic engaged in forensic activity or spoke much in public: Cicero's Brutus makes this clear, even with his very inclusive set of criteria for what

[70] Talbert (1984: 163–184).
[71] Millar (1977: 341–355); Wallace-Hadrill (1982).
[72] Crook (1955: 31–55). Many more decisions were also transmitted in written rather than spoken form: for some of the implications of this, see further Chapter 2.
[73] Tarrant (1984: 460–487); Garnsey (1970: 13–100).
[74] Tacitus, Annals 4.62–63.
[75] See Pliny, Letters 10.3a.

makes a man liable to be considered an orator.[76] Military activity was a feasible, and highly respected, alternate route for public service. But as the equestrian order began to take on some of the activities of senators during the first century A.D. the Senate became a more distinctively civilian organisation and oratory became correspondingly more important for individual senators. This is a change which took a very long time to become clearly established, and in the first century A.D. in particular there were many exceptions. But it is clear that although the status and role of oratory itself was very much the object of scrutiny during this period, and the conclusions drawn about it often pessimistic, the skill of speaking well lost none of its importance for individual members of the elite.

Thus the forms and locations of forensic and deliberative oratory remained very largely in the early Empire as they had been during the Republic, however much the pressures on individual orators in terms of their relationship with their audience may have changed. However, the role of epideictic oratory, the third category of speaking, was fundamentally transformed. Epideictic oratory had a very restricted range of uses during the Republic: only funeral speeches could really be classified as such, though epideictic passages could be used in other kinds of speech.[77] The converse of epideictic, invective, was more widely used, though neither mode of speaking receives much attention in the surviving rhetorical handbooks.[78] However, in the imperial period epideictic has an obvious and compelling object in the form of the emperor.

The first example of panegyric in praise of a sole ruler in Latin is just prior to the imperial period: Cicero's speech *On Behalf of Marcellus*, delivered in 46 B.C.[79] The title, with its suggestion of a forensic case, is misleading. Cicero gave the speech in the Senate without preparation in response to the unexpected agreement of Julius Caesar to allow the return of Gaius Marcellus from exile in Mytilene, where he had been since the battle of Pharsalus. It is not an argument in favour of Marcellus, which would be otiose in the light of Caesar's announcement, and indeed Marcellus is barely mentioned. The speech is concerned rather with the nature of Caesar's rule, particularly his quality of mercy, of which his behaviour towards

---

[76] Steel (2003).
[77] So, for example, the extended praise of Pompeius in Cicero's *On the Command of Gnaeus Pompeius*.
[78] On the uses of invective during the Republic, see further Chapter 3 below.
[79] Dyer (1990); Levene (1997); Winterbottom (2002).

Marcellus is one example; and as well as praising what Caesar has already accomplished Cicero also indicates what he hopes Caesar can be praised for in the future. The speech thus establishes in a remarkably short compass a model of how epideictic oratory can be used programmatically. It also makes Cicero himself as the speaker an important element in the advice which the speech gives: he starts from the fact that Caesar's action has encouraged him to speak because it cannot be allowed to pass in silence, and concludes with emphasising his position both as a spokesman for the assembled Senate and as one who has a personal relationship with both Marcellus and Caesar. The relationship between the speaker of panegyric and the emperor praised continues to be an important aspect of the dynamics of imperial epideictic.[80]

Having delivered this speech Cicero chose also to disseminate a written version. And in the subsequent development of the genre of advice to emperors, oral delivery does not seem essential. Seneca's treatise on Mercy has no pretensions to be a speech, for example; its literary antecedents are rather Hellenistic manuals of advice to kings.[81] Pliny's *Panegyricus* did have an oral outing, but it is quite clear from one of his letters that the written version was an expanded version of what he had said in the Senate.[82] And epideictic oratory receives surprisingly little attention in Quintilian's treatise, a work with clear encyclopaedic aspirations in terms of the coverage of all that Quintilian considers relevant to the orator's task. Morgan has argued that Quintilian's very brief treatment of epideictic should be read as a manifestation of an underlying argument within the *Education of the Orator* about the nature of the orator's political engagement: the essential element is the orator's own moral disposition, and consequently the precise form of government becomes less important.[83] The success of any political system, on this view, is dependent on the virtue of its officers and not on its inherent qualities. From this perspective, Quintilian's reluctance to consider epideictic makes sense as a sign that the particular forms of oratory relevant to an imperial system are not inherent to the job of orator as properly understood. More generally, one could conclude that the relative importance of writing in the dissemination of imperial epideictic is an indication of

[80] Braund (1998).
[81] On Seneca's *On Mercy*, see Griffin (1976: 133–171).
[82] *Letters* 3.18.1.
[83] Morgan (1998).

the marginalisation of occasions of speech as opportunities to articulate the beliefs which underpin the emperor's position.

I have already mentioned in passing some references to Romans using Greek as a medium for oratory outside Rome, though the main focus of this chapter has been on speeches in Latin, delivered in Rome, by members of the Roman elite. In considering epideictic oratory in particular, however, it is arguable that the broadest interpretation of 'Roman oratory', by at least the first century A.D., should also include works written in Greek: the products of a developing Greco-Roman culture in which, increasingly, Greeks are entering the Senate and holding high office whilst maintaining a cultural identity in which the Greek language is paramount. Nonetheless – in addition to inexorable considerations of space – two factors may explain the absence of consideration of the orators of the second sophistic from this book. One is that its impact upon oratory as an element within the government of the Roman state is limited. Latin remains the language of the Roman Senate and of the law-courts in Rome.[84] Four orations on kingship, addressed to Trajan, survive among Dio Chrysostom's speeches; but, unlike Pliny's *Panegyricus*, no delivery in the Senate could be contemplated for them.[85] And secondly, the orators of the second sophistic did not look to Rome for their technical skills, however much Rome and Roman power was a preoccupation in their works.

This survey of oratorical performance at Rome has concentrated on the Republican period because the main forms of oratory are established then, and there is striking continuity, given the massive political changes, in the uses of oratory from the Republican to the Imperial period. The vast majority of our surviving oratorical texts in Latin also date from the Republican period. In the next chapter, I turn to the issues of how and why speeches make the transition from oral delivery to written form.

---

[84] Latin is the language, too, of forensic activity in the western part of the Empire. A remarkable example of forensic oratory from north Africa survives from the middle of the second century A.D.: Apuleius' *Apologia*. This speech is so remarkable, indeed, in its written form that one may wonder how helpful it can be as a guide to forensic practice. Fascinating evidence about the day-to-day level of pleading in Egyptian courts during the period of Roman rule can be found in Heath (2004); see also Crook (1995).

[85] On Dio's kingship orations, see Moles (1983); Konstan (1997); Whitmarsh (2005: 60–63).

II CHANNELS OF COMMUNICATION

The oral dimension to classical literature as a whole has, rightly, become an object of increasing interest to interpreters.[1] The process of composition of any text usually involved a spoken element;[2] public or private readings could be a medium by which a text was disseminated; and individual reading could involve audible speech, or having another person read aloud.[3] All Roman literature involves some oral dimension. Within this broad framework, however, oratory occupies a distinctive space. A speech is prepared for a specific time and place, to be directed at a specific audience and, in the case of forensic and deliberative oratory, with the aim of securing a specific outcome. Moreover, this first performance is, logically, oral and does not imply the existence of a written text; indeed, there was a strong convention within ancient rhetoric that speeches were delivered from memory, and even though written texts might well feature in preparation, orators would often find themselves in situations where improvisation was necessary.[4] The sense of being created for a particular time and place is a characteristic which oratory shares with drama but, unlike drama, subsequent performances in a similar manner are difficult to envisage. Plays in both Greece and Rome were revived after the festival for which they had been initially composed; but the circumstances in front of the Roman people, in the Senate, or in a court which demanded a speech would never be repeated.[5]

A written version of a forensic or deliberative speech, therefore, institutes a new interaction between orator and audience, and the purposes for which a written version of a speech is disseminated can be very different from those which motivated its original delivery. The difference from the occasion of original delivery does not necessarily reside in a transition from heard to read: as we have seen, a written text may be absorbed aurally, and a Roman might well experience the

---

[1] Fantham (1996: 2–11); Watson (2001).

[2] Small (1997: 177–188).

[3] Kenney (1982); Small (1997: 19–25).

[4] See above, Chapter 1.

[5] Cicero's corpus provides examples of speeches being given to different audiences on the same topic and close to one another in time: *To the Citizens after his Recall from Exile* and *To the Senate after his Recall from Exile*, *Philippics* 3 and 4, *Philippics* 5 and 6. Exact repetition of material is not found (Mack 1937); the different audiences required different handling, and on these occasions communication with both was important.

written version of speech produced subsequently to its original delivery by hearing it read aloud to him or her. It depends instead on the responsibilities and capacities of the subsequent reading audience, which, crucially, does not have the opportunity to intervene directly in the debate or trial for which the speech was originally composed. A written speech is not seeking directly to win the approval of its audience, though it may appear to do so if demonstrating the speaker's oratorical skill is a reason why it has been preserved in written form. And a reading audience are also in a position, unlike the original audience, to know the outcome of the trial or debate. Whatever excitement or interest written oratory held for a Roman audience it did not mimic our experience of court-room drama; readers would either know the outcome or, if they did not, the speech itself would not provide it.[6] Verdicts, indeed, are one piece of information which Asconius thinks it worth including in his notes on some of Cicero's speeches.[7]

Our text-based perception of Roman oratory can obscure the fact that written versions of speeches are rather peculiar things which occupy an inescapably secondary position, deriving their origins and much of their meaning from an event of which they are now the only, partial, record. The nature of the record which a written speech provides is also unclear. To what extent is it, or can it be, a verbatim record of what was actually said on the day? Naturally most of the discussion has centred on Cicero.[8] Humbert argued that the nature of Roman court proceedings mean that Cicero's forensic speeches cannot be a verbatim record, as his exposition would be broken up by witness statements and other forms of evidence.[9]

The response to Humbert has often been one of alarm, as though by accepting that a speech is not a script we are utterly cut off from Roman oratory. Yet the implications of Humbert's argument are not so radical. His basic observation about court procedure is undoubtedly correct, and hence Cicero's written version of his forensic speeches must involve an element of tidying-up in order to

---

[6] Quintilian recommends that the aspiring orator should read the speeches on both sides of a forensic case, when these are available (*Education of the Orator* 10.1.22–23); but he has in mind the benefits of knowing a case thoroughly when studying oratory, rather than any cheap dramatic thrills. The fact that Quintilian specifies a few cases where speeches on both side were available might suggest that this was a relatively unusual situation where guidance would be welcome.

[7] Asconius 28C, 53C, 81C.

[8] On the publication of Cicero's speeches specifically, see now the excellent discussion in Powell and Paterson (2004: 52–57).

[9] Humbert (1925: 23–97).

provide a smooth and uninterrupted text.[10] But this text may still reflect reasonably accurately what Cicero said when he was speaking at length.

Humbert identified one reason why this problem exists at all: court procedure would not accommodate unbroken speeches in exactly the form in which Cicero disseminated them. A second reason lies in what we know of orators' writing practices, or rather, lack of them: orators did not use scripts. Indeed, memory was one of the five basic skills of the orator, and it was so crucial precisely because an orator had to have his material memorised ready for use as the situation in court or debate demanded. Quintilian records that Cicero wrote out his perorations and exordia which he then memorised for delivery;[11] these parts of a speech were relatively immune from sudden and unexpected developments. But otherwise, with very rare exceptions, he had only notes. However, the lack of a script does not mean that a speech could not be reconstructed subsequently. A well-prepared orator would not necessarily be making things up as he went along: he would have reflected on the evidence and arguments he would use, the structure of his speech, and the appropriate style; and, one must imagine, have made notes as part of his preparations. All these would be to hand if he decided, after he had delivered his speech, that he wished to put a written version of what he had said into circulation. With a combination of preparation and trained memory, a reasonably accurate record of what was said could be put into written form if the orator so desired.

There are further considerations which suggest that orators might want their written versions to resemble what they said. Stroh put forward a pedagogical argument in his defence of the veracity of Cicero's written versions: Cicero expected his speeches to be read by those aspiring to be orators.[12] We should expect his versions to be useful for such students, and they can only be useful if they offer a reasonable guide to what an orator might actually want to say. Moreover, one does not have to accept that the pedagogical motive was in fact dominant in Cicero's decision to disseminate his speeches to acknowledge its force in relation to accuracy: if he hoped that young men might read his works because they wanted to emulate his skills as an orator then there must be some level at which his written works

---

[10] The texts of some of Cicero's forensic speeches indicate where material from the pleading was left out e.g. *On Behalf of Murena* 57.

[11] Quintilian, *Education of the Orator* 10.7.30.

[12] Stroh (1975: 7–54).

reflect what he did say. More generally, one can argue that by writing down his speeches Cicero is providing a show-case for his brilliance as an orator and ensuring for it a wider and more lasting audience, whether or not part of that audience is going to use the texts as teaching tools. Again, this supports a belief that his written speeches offer a credible guide to what he said.

Some valuable evidence about the relationship between spoken and written speeches occurs in Quintilian.[13] His discussion is prompted by a query from a hypothetical reader as to whether it is appropriate to use epigrams in speeches which are written down, as well as in spoken delivery. Quintilian argues that it is: 'speaking well and writing well are, in my view, one and the same thing'.[14] He presents his opinion as somewhat unorthodox: many critics have argued that the two activities do have different criteria of excellence. And this discussion is concerned primarily with the critical evaluation of written speeches and the reasons why it may be permissible to speak in a different way from how one writes, and not with the very possibility of accurate written record of speeches. Nonetheless, Quintilian writes as though this is a possibility, even if some critics regard verbatim records as a less satisfactory kind of written oratory than one which makes use of different criteria of excellence from those applicable to speaking. He continues the opinion, quoted above, by saying 'and a written speech is nothing other than the record of a spoken case'.[15] Quintilian is not, of course, in a position to comment on the relationship between speech and writing in Cicero's case; indeed, he says of both Cicero and Demosthenes, 'Do we have access to these outstanding speakers in any way other than through their writings?'[16] But it would be strange for Quintilian to have approached the issue in the way that he does if he knew that written speeches in his own day simply did not bear a close relationship to what had been said in court.

It seems, therefore, that Roman critics did not see any impossibility in the idea that a written speech might be an accurate representation of what an orator had said. However, the practicalities of forensic practice mean that the texts we have must involve some degree of tidying up; and it is clear from Quintilian that there were some orators

[13] Quintilian, *Education of the Orator* 12.10.49–57.

[14] Quintilian, *Education of the Orator* 12.10.51, *mihi unum atque idem uidetur bene dicere ac bene scribere.*

[15] Quintilian, *Education of the Orator* 12.10.51, *neque aliud esse oratio scripta quam monumentum actionis habitae.*

[16] Quintilian *Education of the Orator* 12.10.54, *aut eos praestantissimos oratores alia re quam scriptis cognoscimus?*

and critics who believed that a written speech needed to be different from what was said if it were to attain excellence. Moreover, the dissemination of a written version of a speech is not an automatic sequel to the delivery of a speech. A consideration of the development of writing practices in relation to oratory will clarify some of the factors which affect this form.

Cato the Elder appears to have been the first Roman politician to commit his forensic and deliberative speeches to written form.[17] He included texts of some of his speeches in his history, *Origines*; it is not clear whether his speeches circulated independently as well. Cato's innovation was to revisit the occasion of the delivery of a speech and produce a text which purported to be what he said on that occasion. And a striking quotation from one of his speeches from one of Fronto's letters shows him taking the preservation of accurate records very seriously.[18] In it he shows himself going through an earlier speech, listening to passages which are read out to him from it, and deciding that they need not be included in the new speech he is composing.

Cato produced written versions of both deliberative and forensic speeches and, though most of his forensic activity was either prosecution or self-defence, he seems sometimes to have acted as an advocate for another.[19] In relation to forensic oratory, it is worth considering here a familiar distinction between Athenian and Roman legal systems. In Athens, plaintiffs and defendants spoke on their own behalf; at Rome, advocates spoke for defendants, and sometimes also for plaintiffs.[20] Athenian orators wrote speeches for others to deliver as well as delivering speeches themselves and being a *logographos*, a writer of speeches, could be a profitable occupation. Within this environment written texts of speeches are, almost inevitably, brought into existence.[21] But at Rome the job of the *patronus* was not to provide

[17] Q. Fabius Maximus Cunctator is supposed to have had a written version of the funeral speech he delivered for his son disseminated (Cicero, *Cato the Elder* 12). But funeral speeches (*laudationes*) are a distinct category of oratory, intimately connected with wider funeral rites: Kierdorf (1980); Flower (1996: 128–158) and see Chapter 1 above. There are strong grounds for scepticism about the historicity of other surviving quotations from orators before Cato, and even if such texts were to date back to a member of the audience who recorded what he heard, they would still not be the product of the speaker's own decision to produce a written record of what he had said.

[18] Fronto, p. 90 l. 15ff (van den Hout).

[19] Malcovati, frs. 206, 210.

[20] Crook (1995); Powell and Paterson (2004: 10–19).

[21] It is at least conceivable that a *logographos* could instruct his client orally; but there is no evidence to suggest this happened, and one might expect that a client wanted a tangible artefact in return for the (often considerable) sum he would have spent.

the text of a speech for someone else to deliver but to deliver a speech himself.[22] A written text of part or all of the speech may have been part of the advocate's compositional process, but he was under no obligation to provide that text to his client, and his job was purely oral: to deliver a speech in court on a specific day and in relation to a specific case. The transition from spoken to written was thus not an essential part of the legal process at Rome in the way that it had been in Athens, and a Roman orator was always faced with a *choice* of whether or not to produce a written version which could then be disseminated.

There seems to have been an eager market for written forensic oratory at Athens. It is less clear who sought to obtain copies of Cato's speeches and those of his successors who chose also to disseminate written versions, but it is at least possible to hypothesise some important differences in the profile and aims of the Roman reading audience. Any male Athenian citizen could find himself needing to speak on his own behalf in court; the capacity to speak well was potentially of direct and urgent concern, and written speeches could thus offer didactic gains as well as aesthetic pleasure. Ordinary Romans were much less likely to face such demands, since the existence of the patron–client relationship meant, in theory at least, the existence of legal support and advice to which they could turn; and, as discussed in the previous chapter, there were no opportunities to address the citizen body which were open to all citizens. This does not mean that we should assume Romans in general were not interested in oratory: there is plenty of evidence for the presence of crowds of bystanders at big trials, and the exercise of voting rights as a citizen would often involve listening to speeches. But a citizen, unless he had political ambitions or was seeking to make his living from forensic oratory, would not find himself called upon, or even have the opportunity, to speak in public himself. The number of those interested in written oratory at Rome as a source of instruction was likely, therefore, to be much smaller than at Athens.

The existence of advocacy also has a profound effect on the figure of the orator himself within the forensic speeches that he delivered. The character of the advocate becomes a third element in the situation in addition to the characters of plaintiff and defendant. Cicero's forensic speeches demonstrate very clearly the range of persuasive

---

[22] The patron–client relationship could, however, involve ghost-writers: one example is the *eques* L. Aelius Stilo, who wrote speeches for others and thereby acquired his *cognomen*: Suetonius, *On Grammarians and Rhetors* 3.

effects which the deployment of his *persona* could create.[23] The orator's presence within his speeches also contributes to their impact on a reading audience. In an Athenian forensic speech the identity of the author is not immediately obvious, though traits of style may be revealing; and the ascription of surviving forensic speeches is in fact often doubtful. No such obscurity affects Roman forensic oratory, where the identity of the orator is clear, and usually crucial to the strategy of the speech.[24] And, in turn, a speech is not necessarily just a free-standing object, relevant only to a particular trial: if its author has been involved in other trials it can contribute to an evolving public *persona* articulated over a number of speeches.

The existence of advocacy within the Roman legal system has therefore important implications for the relationship between speeches and their written versions: on the one hand it removes the compulsion – in comparison with Athens – to produce a written text, but on the other it offers a clear unity, in the person of the orator, to those speeches which are written down. The importance of the advocate also establishes a link between forensic and deliberative oratory: many politicians were also lawyers, as discussed in the previous chapter, and in such cases might choose to provide written versions of both kinds of oratory.

Cato the elder was one who did so choose, but the writing practices of orators after him are varied, and indicate that dissemination was far from being an uncomplicated activity. The main ancient source for Roman oratory before Cicero is Cicero's own *Brutus*: the structure and overall argument of this history of orators is dominated by Cicero's preoccupations with his own lasting reputation, but there is no good reason to suspect the accuracy of the wealth of detail which he includes.[25] He refers to the existence of written texts of speeches by very many of the orators whom he mentions as active in the period after Cato. However, not all orators appear to have disseminated written versions of their speeches.

In many cases an argument from silence cannot be pressed too far, since written versions disseminated by a minor orator might simply be ignored by subsequent generations. But in some cases we have an explicit reference to the lack of written versions. One such case is that of M. Antonius (consul in 99 B.C. and grandfather of the triumvir).

---

[23] Paterson (2004); May (1988).
[24] This does not preclude forgery. Cicero clearly thought ascription of authorship was sufficiently fragile for its being worth his while to try to deny that he had written an attack on Clodius and Curio when political priorities changed (Cicero, *Letters to Atticus* 3.12.2).

According to Cicero in his defence of Cluentius, Antonius would say 'he had never written down a speech so that he could deny having said something if it was later unhelpful for him to have said it'.[26] His contemporary Crassus, who did have written versions of some of his deliberative speeches disseminated, faced a variation on this problem in a forensic case, when his opponent read out contradictory parts of two of Crassus' speeches, in one of which he defended the position of the Senate and in the other sought to diminish its authority.[27] When Cicero discusses the question in *Brutus* he offers a number of other explanations for the failure of some orators to write down their speeches:

> We observe that other orators have written nothing through laziness, so as not to add work at home to their efforts in court – and most speeches are written down having already been delivered, not so they can be delivered; and that others don't work hard in order to improve – for nothing so benefits speaking as composition: but they don't want to leave a record of their skill for posterity, as they think they have already acquired enough glory from speaking and that it will seem all the greater if their writings are not subjected to the judgement of critics; and others don't because they think they can speak better than they can write – which does happen often in the case of highly intelligent people who aren't particularly educated . . .[28]

It is clear from this passage that producing written versions of speeches was a separate activity from delivering a speech and not just an extension of the same process: it required considerable extra effort and, to a certain extent, a different set of skills – as the passage of Quintilian discussed above also suggests. And even those orators who did choose to create and disseminate a written version did not necessarily do so for every speech which they delivered. Three speeches only of Ser. Sulpicius Galba, whom Cicero identifies as one of the leading orators of the mid-second century B.C., survived as far as Livy knew; but he gives a detailed account of a further occasion when Galba spoke against L. Aemilius Paullus' being awarded a triumph; and Cicero describes how he defended some *publicani* against a charge

---

[25] Gowing (2000); Steel (2003).

[26] Cicero, *On Behalf of Aulus Cluentius* 140, *idcirco se nullam umquam orationem scripsisse ut, si quid aliquando non opus esset ab se esse dictum, posset negare dixisse.*

[27] Cicero, *On Behalf of Aulus Cluentius* 140–141; *On the Orator* 2.223–5.

[28] Cicero, *Brutus* 91–92, *nam uidemus alios oratores inertia nihil scripsisse, ne domesticus etiam labor accederet ad forensem – pleraeque enim scribuntur orationes habitae iam, non ut habeantur –; alios non laborare, ut meliores fiant – nulla enim res tantum ad dicendum proficit quantum scriptio –: memoriam autem in posterum ingeni sui non desiderant, cum se putant satis magnam adeptos esse dicendi gloriam eamque etiam maiorem uisum iri, si in existimantium arbitrium sua scripta non uenerint; alios, quod melius putent dicere se posse quam scribere, quod peringeniosis hominibus neque satis doctis plerumque contingit.*

that their slaves had committed murder.[29] Crassus published only a few of his speeches, and none of his forensic ones, despite his pre-eminence among orators of his generation.[30]

So when Cicero delivered his first speech in public, in 81 B.C., he was immediately faced with the issue of whether or not to have a written version disseminated: the writing practices of earlier orators had firmly established the possibility of doing so, though it was in no way an automatic sequel to having delivered a speech.[31] His first speech was not perhaps an obvious candidate for such treatment: it was a civil law speech, concerning a dispute over the ownership of property in Gaul.[32] The litigants were obscure and the case itself not particularly interesting. On the other hand, the advocate for the opposing side was Hortensius, already one of the leading advocates of the period despite his relative youth: the civil wars of the 80s had led to the deaths of many of the oratorical talents of the previous generation. His presence gave the case added interest. This would be particularly true if Cicero's client Quinctius had won the case; but there is no evidence on this point. But the most compelling argument for dissemination is Cicero's desire for an audience. He had already written part of a textbook on rhetoric, On Invention, which shows ambition beyond its scale in its reflections on the role of oratory in civilised society.[33] Now finally he had made his debut as an orator; and he could not at this stage know how soon the next commission would arrive.

His subsequent dissemination practices show that simple advertisement was an important, though not overwhelming, consideration early in his career when he published a relatively high proportion of the speeches which he delivered: given that he was not getting a very great deal of business, he seems to have been eager to produce written versions wherever possible.[34] But in the sixties, as he held high public office, he started to have the opportunity to deliver deliberative

[29] Livy 45.35.8; Cicero, Brutus 85–7.
[30] Cicero, On the Orator 132.
[31] Cicero's dissemination practices are considered in detail by J. Crawford (1984, 1994).
[32] For details of the case, see Kinsey (1971).
[33] Steel (2005: 34–40); see further below, Chapter 4.
[34] Eight forensic speeches delivered in Rome can be identified and definitely placed during the first decade of Cicero's career as an orator: i.e. slightly fewer than one a year. He had written versions of four disseminated (On Behalf of Publius Quinctius, On Behalf of Sextus Roscius, On Behalf of Varenus and On Behalf of Tullius). Of the other four, one defence was unsuccessful (that of Scamander) which probably explains why no version of this speech was written up; reasons for his silence in the other cases (a defence of a woman from Arretium and on behalf of Titinia and of Mustius) are unclear.

speeches, and many of these are disseminated in written form; there is a particular concern for the speeches from his year as consul. In the 50s he was extremely busy in the courts, but wrote up a much smaller proportion of these forensic cases, and in particular did not preserve those occasions where he defended people at the pressing behest of Pompeius or Caesar.[35] The three Caesarian speeches from the period of Caesar's dictatorship mark an attempt to formulate an oratory which could be effective in an autocracy; and by the time he delivers the *Philippics* written dissemination is as important as oral delivery, given that power is now fragmented across Rome's territorial empire.

The sheer quantity of Cicero's surviving speeches, and the paucity of those from other orators, make him the central case study in looking at the writing practices of Roman orators during the Republican period. In the rest of this chapter I shall look at two sets of material from the imperial period which demonstrate further manifestations of the relationship between oratory and writing: one relates to the younger Pliny and the other to the circumstances of speaking to and listening to the emperor.

The younger Pliny (c. A.D. 61– c. A.D. 112) was one of the leading orators of his generation with a busy legal practice; and he disseminated versions of many of his speeches. Only one of them survives: the *Panegyricus*, his speech in praise of Trajan from A.D. 100. But since this is one of only two surviving complete examples of Roman speeches which are not by Cicero, Pliny is an important figure.[36] Moreover, his profile as an orator can be traced in some detail in the first nine books of his *Letters*. Indeed, Mayer has recently argued that the references to oratory in the letters are 'both a carefully planned campaign of advertisement and an insurance policy': Pliny uses his letters to increase the chances that his written speeches will secure for him lasting *gloria*.[37]

Mayer's observations on the effect that the letters may have been intended to have on the speeches can be supplemented in turn by a consideration of the role that references to oratory play in Pliny's letters. References to oratory – whether Pliny's or that of other people – occur extremely frequently. His letters allow us to flesh out the variety of occasions on which a successful public servant might find himself required to speak in public. But Pliny's interest is not limited to recording his own performances. He is very interested in the

---

[35] Steel (2005: 21–28).
[36] The other is Apuleius' *Apologia*.
[37] Mayer (2003: 232).

transition from spoken to written for oratorical performances in general, and he is also keen to demonstrate his critical awareness of the works of others. To take the second book of letters as an example: there are twenty letters, and oratory is mentioned in some guise in six of them.[38] Two relate to Pliny's writing up of his own speeches, two to his forensic practice, and two to the oratory of others.

Letter 2.5 purports to accompany a copy of a speech Pliny made at the opening of a library in his home town of Comum, which he is sending to Lupercus in partial draft for editing suggestions; 2.19 is a discussion of whether Pliny should give a reading of a speech he delivered in court. These two are examples of the parallel narratives, of letter and of speech, which Mayer discusses: in both cases, the letter tells the reader about the speech, thereby advertising its presence and providing a substitute in case the letter-reader does not want also to read the written version of the speech. But these letters also assume an interested audience. Both demand some prior knowledge from the reader if s/he is to identify which speech Pliny is referring to, since his descriptions are oblique: in 2.5 it is 'the speech which you have frequently asked for and I often promised';[39] in 2.19 it is described in the first sentence simply as 'the speech', and only halfway through does Pliny offer further description: 'the speech which I'm talking about is aggressive, almost quarrelsome'.[40] These letters operate as a supplement to Pliny's published oratory only in very general terms: they indicate his forensic activity and they give a flavour of his performance. This lack of detail does not, of course, preclude readers who will know exactly what Pliny is referring to. Pliny's efforts at memorialisation at this point are thus to do with the act of being a busy forensic speaker and not with the details of his practice. This approach avoids excessive detail about cases which might in themselves not be particularly interesting as well as creating the impression that everyone does, in fact, follow his performances with such attention that they can understand the sketchy references without difficulty.

Letter 2.14 is also very general: it deals with the behaviour of advocates and audiences in the centumviral court, where much of Pliny's forensic practice was located. Moreover, it is an extended complaint:

---

[38] Pliny, *Letters* 2.1, 2.3, 2.5, 2.11, 2.14, 2.19.

[39] Pliny, *Letters* 2.5.1, *Actionem et a te frequenter efflagitatam, et a me saepe promissam.*

[40] Pliny, *Letters* 2.19.5, *Accedit his quod oratio de qua loquor pugnax et quasi contentiosa est.* Modern readers do not possess such knowledge, at least not to the extent of certainty: see Sherwin-White (1966: 150–151, 202).

about the triviality of the cases, the poor quality of the advocates and
of their oratory; and the raucous behaviour of hired claqueurs. Pliny
presents his own appearances there as a matter of duty towards his
friends and his own public image. One way of interpreting this letter
is as an exculpation of limited public approbation of his performances
at the centumviral court. If he himself was not normally greeted by
enthusiasm from the crowd, then an explanation that such enthusiasm
was generated by cash rather than outstanding performances could
explain away apparent failure. But this may be too literal an interpretation. Pliny's letter is setting up two different forms of appreciation
for oratory. One is the audience he describes, who 'don't understand
and don't even listen' and whose applause is purchased at established
rates.[41] The second consists initially of Maximus, the letter's
addressee, and then its subsequent readers who, like Pliny, deplore the
debasement of popular judgement and can appreciate Pliny's histori-
cally informed analysis of the current situation. It is a letter about the
judgement of oratory which establishes an implicit hierarchy of critical responses; but it is also a letter about spoken oratory rather than
about a written text.

Letter 2.11 is more specific, and more weighty. It provides a long
description of the prosecution in the Senate of a former governor of
Africa, in which Pliny and Tacitus were the prosecutors. The climax
was a three-day session in the Senate, in the presence of the emperor
Trajan, during which Pliny and Tacitus spoke as prosecutors, three
defenders responded, and, on the third day, the Senate debated the
appropriate penalty and at least two consulars spoke at length. Pliny
characterises and commends the oratory of Tacitus and of two of the
defenders and also describes his own apprehension before speaking
and the kindly response of the emperor to his efforts. It is a very good
example of Pliny's use of letters to secure oratorical *gloria* and it also
gives an indication of what Pliny thought was important to record for
posterity in relation to his speaking. One point is that he is not overly
concerned with technical details. It is not immediately clear from the
letter that the whole judicial process is spread over the best part of
eighteen months; nor does Pliny refer in this letter to his appeal to the
emperor Trajan as to whether he should pay attention to the Senate's
request of him that he be included in the ballot for advocates for this
case, despite the fact that he had decided not to be active in the courts
at this time while he held the post of prefect of the Treasury of

---

[41] Pliny, *Letters* 2.14.7, *non intellegentes, ne audientes quidem.*

Saturn.[42] Pliny constructs 2.11 rather to focus on the occasion of his performance: in a crowded Senate, prosecuting a distinguished man, and in front of the emperor. The relative importance of the speakers can be gauged from the amount of time Pliny devotes to each: a lengthy paragraph on his own performance is in contrast to the single – though polite – sentences devoted to the other advocates. A final point to be made about this letter is that we do not know with certainty that Pliny ever wrote up a version of his prosecution of Marius Priscus. If he did not, then the record in the letter is not an alternative to the speech itself, but a substitute for it.

So far, Pliny has been reflecting upon his own oratory. Twice in the second book of letters he engages in sustained criticism of another's speaking. Letter 2.3 is a straightforward account of the declamation of the sophist Isaeus, showing Pliny's critical acumen and acting as a peg for some further literary anecdotes.[43] Isaeus' job, though, is to create pleasure: what he does is a direct contrast to 'those of us who wear ourselves out in the forum with real cases'.[44] In 2.1, however, Pliny critiques a rival. The letter as a whole is a response to the recent death of Verginius Rufus, and includes a description of the funeral and of the speech delivered there by Tacitus. But Pliny has silently upstaged Tacitus by surrounding the note of Tacitus' performance with his own quasi-funeral oration for Verginius. The opening section of the letter gives a summary of Verginius' life; then, after recording Tacitus as the giver of the funeral speech, Pliny then immediately moves to more emotional reflections upon the loss: 'we must be conscious of the loss of a model of the previous generation, and I above all miss him', and then goes on to explain why his earlier relations with Verginius heighten his grief now.[45] The impression is clear: Tacitus may have delivered the actual speech, because he was consul, but Pliny was the one truly qualified to do so in terms of his relationship with the dead man.[46] In this letter Pliny uses the occasion of *another's* speech to attempt to establish his own pre-eminence as an orator.

One of the things which oratory seems to do in the letters is to bind together different aspects of Pliny's character. Talking about oratory allows him to demonstrate his critical acumen and his mastery of a

---

[42] Pliny, *Letters* 10.3a.

[43] Isaeus was a sophist from Syria (Philostratus, *Lives of the Sophists* 74); Juvenal uses him as an example of a contemporary Greek sophist (3.74).

[44] Pliny, *Letters* 2.3.4, *nos enim, qui in foro uerisque litibus terimur.*

[45] Pliny, *Letters* 2.1.7, *nobis tamen quaerendus ac desiderandus est ut exemplar aeui prioris, mihi uero praecipue.*

[46] Note in particular 2.1.9, where Pliny claims a quasi-filial position in relation to Verginius.

range of literary and historical anecdote: it thus provides a link to his other literary and cultural interests. But it is also a skill which he regularly uses in the performance of his public duties. We have seen in Chapter 1 how the locations for oratory remained remarkably unchanged from Republic to Empire. And oratory retained immense cultural prestige. But it had lost its importance as a catalyst for great events, at least in the opinion of some commentators. We could see in Pliny's letters a new solution to the problem of recording oratory which reflects a changing set of needs to be fulfilled by the dissemination of written versions. If oratory is no longer the means by which matters of profound public concern are articulated, and is instead devoted to legal and administrative matters of limited interest to those not immediately involved, then the texts of such speeches may not secure posterity's lasting interest. Nor does Pliny necessarily need posterity to know the details of his activities as orator for his reputation as a speaker to be secured. A brief, lively summary will test a reader's patience less, while keeping Pliny's status as an orator firmly in our attention. And so, in addition to letters which refer to written speeches, there are those letters which describe the environment and Pliny's own performance in cases where a written text was perhaps not ever produced. Some letters act as parallels to speeches and advertisements for them; others take the place of the written version, which has remained unwritten; and yet more offer us Pliny as the critic of others' speeches.

The letter form is thus much more flexible than the written speech, as it had developed at Rome. Letters can give verdicts, audience responses, and what the other advocates did, all of which are inevitably absent from a speech text. And letters about speaking can be placed next to letters on a whole range of subjects, so establishing oratory as one of a whole range of activities in which Pliny, as an exemplar of a Roman senator, is engaged.[47] As elements in his planned campaign of self-glorification, the letters work alongside his speeches as mutually reinforcing narratives. But perhaps, as a letter-writer, Pliny was more prescient than he knew. The speeches, with the exception of the *Panegyricus*, have perished; the letters have survived.

The second area I explore in this chapter relates to methods of communication with the emperor. The effects of the transformation of Rome's political system from oligarchy to monarchy on the role of

---

[47] See now the collection of essays in *Arethusa* 36(2) (2003).

oratory in politics are discussed in Chapter 1. This change is usually seen as deleterious to the quality of oratory, a view articulated with compelling force in Tacitus' *Dialogus*.[48] Nonetheless, the change did create a new category of speech and of its written record: how to speak to the emperor and how, in turn, the emperor might speak to his subjects. Speech is however only one element within these patterns of interaction. The distinction between formal oratory and other forms of oral communication become blurred in the written records, as emperors and others attempt to create effective ways of speaking to one another and to posterity.

Formal oratorical addresses to the emperor come under the heading of panegyric. Most of the surviving prose panegyrics date from the third and fourth centuries and are beyond the scope of this book: only Pliny's *Panegyricus* from A.D. 100 offers an earlier example. But the roots of the panegyric style go back well into the Republican period.[49] As I discussed in the previous chapter, the dead were praised in funeral speeches, part of the elaborate rituals of commemoration surrounding aristocratic burials that also fed into the competitive culture among the living. Aristocratic competition made invective rather than panegyric the more familiar mode amongst the living but Cicero's corpus includes examples of panegyric writing which are markers of the changing political methods that created the need for extravagant praise of the living.[50]

Praise of the emperor became a familiar aspect of senatorial debate in the imperial period and on some occasions was a formal duty, as Pliny makes clear in describing the circumstances of his delivery of his *Panegyricus*.[51] But a speech was not the only means by which a Roman might seek to address his emperor. A whole range of kinds of literature was dedicated to the emperor.[52] In most cases this merely expressed the writer's hope for or repayment of patronage, but some works seem to have attempted more specific communication, such as Seneca's *On Mercy* where the message on mercy is very clearly directed at the new emperor Nero. The nature of imperial power meant that talking to the emperor did not necessarily require a public

[48] Gowing (2005: 109–120).

[49] Braund (1998).

[50] *On Behalf of Marcellus* is discussed in Chapter 1; and *On Behalf of Ligarius* and *On Behalf of King Deiotarius* are also composed to take account of Caesar's autocratic power (Gotoff 1993: xxix–lx; Gotoff 2002; Johnson 2004).

[51] Pliny, *Letters* 3.18.1.

[52] For example, the elder Pliny's *Natural History* is dedicated to Titus, and Martial turns to Domitian for patronage.

forum and a formal oration – though the opportunity to give such a
speech might be read as one of the benefits of Trajan's reign, in
contrast to that of Domitian. Pliny's concern for the written memo-
rials of his oratory, both in the *Panegyricus* itself and in his
correspondence, demonstrates the continuing importance of oratory
as a marker of status among the elite; and it remained not unusual for
orators to arrange for the dissemination of written versions of their
speeches, though Pliny's is the only one which survives other than in
fragments. A new element, however, is the written record of what
emperors themselves said.

Emperors varied considerably in the importance which they placed
on oratory, both in terms of their own skills and in the amount of time
which they devoted to hearing and delivering oratory. Suetonius
includes a mention of oratory in most of his biographies of the first
twelve emperors and in some cases his remarks are quite detailed,
discussing both composition and offering quotations from speeches.[53]
There is also evidence that imperial oratory survived in inscriptional
form: a famous example is the emperor Claudius' speech to the
Senate on the senatorial ambitions of the inhabitants of Gallia
Comata.[54] Tacitus includes a version of the same speech in the *Annals*
(11.23–4) and comparison of the two has provoked much interest.
But the existence of a Tacitean rewriting can distract from the interest
of Claudius' own speech. The inscription survives only in part; if we
had the whole thing, the emperor Claudius could enter that very
narrow canon of post-Ciceronian orators for whom a speech survives
entire.

The speech combines two separate lines of argument. One is an
explicit claim that the Roman state has always innovated where necessary: 'please rather consider the number of innovations in our
community and the range of forms and structures which our state has
adopted from the very foundation of the city'.[55] Claudius backs this
claim up with a survey of Roman history which takes in the kings, the
transition to Republic, and a range of constitutional innovations
during the Republic, including the dictatorship, the tribunate of the
people, the decemvirate and the extension of office-holding to the
plebeians. Hence there should be no difficulty in making the further

---

[53] Suetonius, *Life of Julius Caesar* 6, 55; *Life of Augustus* 84, 86; *Life of Tiberius*, 8, 70; *Life of Caligula* 53; *Life of Nero* 7; *Life of Titus* 4.

[54] ILS 212; Smallwood (1967) no. 369.

[55] 4–7, *illa potius cogitetis, quam multa in hac ciuitate nouata sint, et quidem statim ab origine urbis nostrae in quot formas statusque res p. nostra diducta sit.*

constitutional innovation of allowing men from Gallia Comata to seek
senatorial office in Rome. The second line of argument that Claudius
implies is that there is no danger to Rome in so doing: the inhabitants
of Gallia Comata can safely be given this honour. They will make
good senators, just as men from Narbonese Gaul have done for many
years; and their province has been peaceful for 100 years, since its
conquest by Julius Caesar, and remained so even during the
campaigns of Claudius' father Drusus against the Germans. Furthermore, Claudius' account of early Roman history records the allegedly
non-Roman origins of many of the kings: 'Kings once controlled this
city, but it was not the case that they handed it down to homegrown
successors'.[56] Numa was a Sabine; Tarquinus Priscus came to Rome
because his talents were denied at Tarquinii; and Servius Tullius was
either the son of a slave or – according to the Etruscans – an Etruscan
warlord originally known as Mastarna.

There are aspects of Claudius' speech that one could criticise.
There are digressions which don't appear to aid the overall argument,
such as the reference to the (unnamed) Valerius Asiaticus: this allu-
sion actually undermines Claudius' case, because he is – as far at least
as Claudius is concerned – an example of an unworthy senator from
Narbonese Gaul, at the point in the speech where he is trying to
establish an argument by analogy, that Narbonese Gaul has produced
good senators and so Gallia Comata will too. The exhortation to
himself, to hurry up, has been criticised as inept; it is always very difficult to determine how humour on the page might go down with a
particular audience, though Suetonius records that Claudius' humour
didn't always work.[57] But, overall, this is an effective as well as a
revealing piece. And Claudius seems to have spoken fairly briefly.
This speech is one belonging to an emperor who is comfortable to be
participating in a debate in the Senate and who demonstrates his
respect to the Senate and its nominal freedom of debate and decision.

The circumstances of its preservation, inscribed on a tablet at
Lyon, are also significant. This town was the location of the annual
meeting of the *concilium Gallorum* and the impetus to make a perma-
nent record of the speech is more likely to have come from the Gauls
than from the emperor himself, though one imagines his permission
might have been sought before the inscription was set up. A community is here commemorating an occasion on which local affairs were a

---

[56] ILS 212, ll. 8–9, *quondam reges hanc tenuere urbem, nec tamen domesticis successoribus eam tradere contigit.*

[57] Suetonius, *Life of Claudius* 21.5. Griffin (1982: 406) refers to 'clumsy imperial jokes'.

matter of discussion in Rome and when the outcome was favourable to them. The emperor had spoken to the Senate in Rome, but his words were subsequently communicated, through an inscription, to a further audience for whom his speech had a serious personal interest.

So far, so straightforward; the Lyon tablet is another example of the capacity of a written speech to transcend the limits not simply of time but also of space imposed on the original delivery. But there are important respects in which this written version is not the same as those I have considered so far in this chapter. Acquiring a copy of a speech of Cicero is a personal matter by an individual reader. It may involve expense or incur an obligation; and it is reasonable to assume that it represents some desire on the part of the person who acquires it to read it. The Lyon tablet, by contrast, is public; it is available to all who happen to be by it without cost, and its public location may in fact work against its content being read. Its importance for those who put it up resides, we might argue, primarily in the fact of its delivery and in the results which followed from its delivery, namely the extension of the opportunity to join the Senate to the inhabitants of long-haired Gaul. The circumstances of its display thus introduce a new element of communication which goes alongside the communication through its words. In spoken oratory, a whole range of extra-textual communication takes place: location, appearance, gesture, audience response all combine with the words to create a total impression. These extra-textual cues are lost when the speech is confined to written form; but if the transition is to inscriptional written form, then another rhetoric is invoked: the placing of the inscription, its relation to other inscriptions or images, the quality of its materials and lettering, and so on.

These extra-textual cues depend on the inscribed form and not on the words' original status as a speech. To that extent, therefore, the Lyon tablet is parallel not to other written speeches, but other inscriptions recording the emperor's voice as pronounced in the form of an edict or letter.[58] The unifying factors are the public display of the text and the authority of the first-person. The epitome of this form of communication could be considered to be Augustus' *Res Gestae*: neither edict, letter, nor speech, it transcends generic categories and the constraints of time and space as it is replicated throughout the Empire, enabling the emperor to speak to all his subjects.[59] The

---

[58] Benner (1975).
[59] Ramage (1987); Bosworth (1999).

nature of the emperor's position thus liberates his words from the constraints of form: they do not need the authority bestowed by the occasion of oratorical performance to make them worth heeding.

During the Republican period, the orator was faced with a choice when he had delivered a speech, but it was a straightforward choice: should he or should he not create a written version of what he had said and allow it to circulate. The impulse to memorialise oratory persisted into the imperial period; but the changing impact of oratory, and above all the distorting presence of the emperor, made other forms of recording oratory attractive.

III THE PRACTISING ORATOR

We have already seen how public speaking was central, during the Republican period, to the operation of the Roman state; and how, despite radical political change between Republic and Empire, oratory retained its position as a key skill for the politically active elite. The importance of oratory made it, in turn, both the vehicle of and the focus for sustained critiques of the behaviour and values of Rome in general and the elite in particular. In this chapter I turn to the figure of the orator and consider how the expectations concerning his behaviour are set up. Technical works on rhetoric, anecdotes about individual orators and surviving oratorical texts can supplement surviving texts of speeches in the task of establishing what the Romans thought their speakers should do and be and how they criticised those who failed to meet these criteria.[1]

The importance of oratory among the tasks which an elite Roman male was expected to be able to undertake can be demonstrated some time before the development of rhetorical theory at Rome. An account survives of part of the funeral speech for L. Caecilius Metellus, delivered by his son Quintus in 221 B.C.:

Quintus Metellus says that . . . he achieved the ten greatest and best things, which wise men spend their lives pursuing: for he wanted to be the foremost warrior, the best speaker, the bravest general, to achieve great things under his own command, to obtain the highest offices, to display outstanding wisdom, to be considered the leading senator, to get great wealth respectably, to leave many children and to be the most distinguished member of his community; and these fell to his lot, as to no other since the foundation of Rome.[2]

Lucius Metellus' outstanding qualities are drawn from warfare, political life and private household affairs: oratory is not at the head of the list, but it is the first civilian skill to be listed. The three-fold division of war, peace and one's family covers everything which a Roman male might pride himself on in these circumstances, though Metellus' specific ten are not canonical. The elder Cato, according to the elder

---

[1] See Burnand (2000); Habinek (2005: 16–37).

[2] Pliny the elder, *Natural History* 7.139, *Q. Metellus ...decem maximas res optimasque, in quibus quaerendis sapientes aetatem exigerent, consummasse eum: uoluisse enim primarium bellatorem esse, optimum oratorem, fortissimum imperatorem, auspicio suo maximas res geri, maximo honore uti, summa sapientia esse, summum senatorem haberi, pecuniam magnam bono modo inuenire, multos liberos relinquere et clarissimum in ciuitate esse. haec contigisse ei nec ulli alii post Romam conditam.*

Pliny in the same section of the *Natural History*, 'is reckoned to have been the first in the Porcian family to have secured the three outstanding human achievements: being the best orator, the best general and the best senator'.[3] P. Licinius Crassus Mucianus, the consul of 131 B.C., was celebrated by historians under five headings: great wealth, great family, outstanding eloquence, unrivalled knowledge of the law, and holding the office of *pontifex maximus*.[4] In the highly competitive world of the mid- and late Republic, such career summaries were carefully constructed to reflect the pinnacles of the honorand's achievements and his distinctive strengths. But eloquence, it seems, was always worth claiming if the claim could in any way be substantiated.

There is an extended argument for the pre-eminence of oratory among civilian skills in a speech which Cicero delivered in 63 B.C. in defence of one of the consuls-elect for 62 B.C., L. Licinius Murena. The election campaign during the summer of 63 for the consulship of the following year had been unusually tense, with four serious contenders in the field, including Catilina.[5] Bribery was taking place so extensively during the campaign that Cicero, as consul, proposed, successfully, a law which substantially increased the penalties for this activity and it was under this law that Murena was charged.[6] Ser. Sulpicius, one of the unsuccessful candidates, and the younger Cato were among the prosecutors.[7] Much of Cicero's defence is concerned with an appeal to the safety of the state at a time of crisis, which requires that there be two consuls in office at the beginning of 62 B.C., and with a defence of himself in the face, it seems, of prosecution attacks on his influence.[8] Insofar as he does offer a defence on the bribery charge he does so by arguing that Murena had no need to use bribery, as he was a much more attractive candidate than Sulpicius and therefore would have been elected without such aid. This attractiveness lay in the fact that Murena was primarily a soldier, whereas

---

[3] Pliny, *Natural History* 7.100, *Cato primus Porciae gentis tres summas in homine res praestitisse existimatur, ut esset optimus orator, optimus imperator, optimus senator*...Cf. Nepos, *Cato* 3.1.

[4] Aulus Gellius 1.13.10, *Is Crassus a Sempronio Asellione et plerisque aliis historiae Romanae scriptoribus traditur habuisse quinque rerum bonorum maxima et paecipua: quod esset ditissimus, quod nobilissimus, quod eloquentissimus, quod iuris consultissimus, quod pontifex maximus*. This is the Crassus whose skills as a speaker of numerous dialects of Greek also impressed his contemporaries; see Chapter 1.

[5] In addition to Catilina, Ser. Sulpicius Rufus, D. Iunius Silanus and L. Licinius Murena were all plausible candidates.

[6] On the *lex Tullia de ambitu*, see Lintott (1990); Yakobson (1999: 26–43).

[7] On the *Murena*, see Leeman (1982); Classen (1985: 120–179); Riggsby (1999: 21–49).

[8] See Paterson (2004: 89–91).

Sulpicius was a legal expert: 'who can doubt that a reputation acquired through military activity brings much more weight to a consular campaign than that obtained in civil law?'.[9] But Cicero does not simply pit military against legal skill. He also introduces oratory – as the only fitting civilian counterpart to the soldier. Military skill remains at the apex of citizen achievement, but second place is held by skill in speaking rather than skill in the law: oratory can direct affairs of state, and enables the orator to secure friendship and support. It thus fulfils the two criteria necessary to make a skill attractive to the Roman people: it is prestigious, and it is useful.[10] 'There is none of these in that knack of yours, Sulpicius'.[11]

Cicero had no need to bring oratory into this part of the argument at all: a straight comparison between military and legal activity would have sufficed to show that Murena was a more attractive candidate than Sulpicius. His inclusion of oratory relates rather to his own prominence within this speech, and the consul who can 'put down tribunician madness, divert an excited crowd, and stand up to state handouts' is to be seen as exemplified by Cicero himself.[12] The argument overall can hardly be taken as an indication of the unassailable pre-eminence of oratory in the minds of Romans generally. And Cicero could undoubtedly have produced a highly convincing argument in support of the thesis that legal experts were pre-eminent, had ever a case demanded this of him, or indeed that oratory was pernicious. The significance of the argument in *On Behalf of Murena* lies rather in the kinds of attractiveness which Cicero posits as belonging to the orator. Oratory, whilst subordinate to military skill, is nonetheless comparable to it in terms of its importance within the civilian sphere, and the orator's sound deployment of his skills lies at the heart of the well-run state.[13] The collaboration of orator and soldier for the good of the state is a concept which Cicero returned to soon after this speech, as he prepared for the return of Pompeius from the East.[14]

---

[9] *On Behalf of Murena* 22, *qui potest dubitari quin ad consulatum adipiscendum multo plus adferat dignitatis rei militaris quam iuris ciuilis gloria?* On 'legal expert' – *iurisconsultus* – see Frier (1985).

[10] *On Behalf of Murena* 24.

[11] *On Behalf of Murena* 24, *quorum in isto uestro artificio, Sulpici, nihil est.*

[12] *On Behalf of Murena* 24, *consul qui dicendo non numquam comprimat tribunicios furores, qui concitatum populum flectat, qui largitioni resistat.*

[13] *On Behalf of Murena* 30 puts the two in clear parallel: 'There are two skills which can place men at the top of the political ladder: one of them, that of the general, and the other that of the good orator. The latter maintains the benefits of peace and the former repels the dangers of war.' (*duae sunt artes quae possint locare homines in amplissimo gradu dignitatis, una imperatoris, altera oratoris boni. ab hoc enim pacis ornamenta retinentur, ab illo belli pericula repelluntur.*)

[14] Steel (2005: 49–63).

The changing role of oratory in the imperial period seems to have had relatively little impact on the importance of the skill to individual members of the elite: it retained a great deal of prestige. Indeed, it seems that oratory may have become a more important skill for members of the Senate as a whole: as discussed in Chapter 1, during the first century A.D. their role increasingly involved forensic activity and was becoming, albeit with many exceptions, more civilian and less military in its scope. Consequently, a situation developed in which oratory in front of large audiences as a whole had clearly lost a great deal of its importance as a tool in influencing political outcomes; but it remained a skill which was of great importance for individual members of the elite to possess, and be seen to possess.

The younger Pliny's concern in his letters is one example of the contribution which oratory could make to one senator's reputation during this period. Another nice example is that of Rutilius Gallicus, a distinguished public figure in the latter part of the first century A.D. who is excessively well-known to posterity because a lengthy inscription recording the earlier part of his career and a poem by Statius celebrating his recovery from illness both survive.[15] Rutilius' career was largely military and involved lengthy service outside Rome: he served in Pannonia and Galatia and was governor of Asia, though his final office was as prefect of the city. And his military achievements are prominent among the qualities Statius praises. But he also describes Rutilius as 'immense and distinguished in eloquence',[16] and brings in his capacity as a speaker in the passage where he appeals to Rutilius himself to be the source of Statius' poetic inspiration.[17]

It is this importance of public speaking as an aristocratic skill which, in part, explains the intense scrutiny on orators and oratory within Roman culture. But in the Republican period there is another compelling reason why oratory draws such attention: the act of public speaking is one of the occasions at which members of the elite were visible. Roman politics during the Republic was a public business, and politicians needed to demonstrate their activity through regular performance. Tribunes of the people had, of course, to be accessible at all hours. Others in public life were supposed to be available, when in Rome, at the early morning *salutatio*; and if they subsequently went down into the Forum they could expect to be approached for aid and

---

[15] Statius, *Siluae* 1.4; ILS 9499; Henderson (1998).
[16] Statius, *Siluae* 1.4.71–2, *clarus et ingens/eloquio.*
[17] Statius, *Siluae* 1.4.19–36.

advice. Carelessness or inattentiveness in fulfilling these expectations, particularly at election time, made an exceedingly bad impression on the Roman people, and famous instances of such behaviours became exemplary.[18] Roman politicians had to be exceedingly careful about what they said in public as well as what they did.

The intense public scrutiny of politicians during the Republic when they were at Rome nonetheless left some opportunities for privacy. Not all were welcome. Cicero laments the lack of attention that is paid to achievements outside Rome in his speech *On Behalf of Plancius*, in a passage of autobiography in which he explains that he was so disappointed that his quaestorship in Lilybaeum made no impression on anybody at Rome that he thereafter determined to centre his career at Rome.[19] But at Rome, too, some areas were private. Morstein-Marx has recently argued that all politicians who attempted to persuade the people did so by appealing to a set of shared attitudes to popular power.[20] The contest at the *contio*, on this view, was not between fundamentally opposed views of what the people could and could not do: it was between different individual politicians each claiming to uphold the popular will more truly and effectively than his opponent. Modern readers are in a privileged position in relation to Cicero's original contional audience: we know, from his letters and philosophical works along with his speeches, that his overall stance was firmly optimate. But the picture which emerges from his speeches to the people is of a politician firmly committed to the dignity and standing of the Roman people. The 'man in the street' would have no access to Cicero's private views on the Roman people. Morstein-Marx calls this gap between contional and overall *persona* the 'invisible optimate'; and he is surely correct to draw attention to the possibility in the Republic of such fissured self-presentations. The good orator could indeed be all things to all men; the problem for Cicero arose when he had to take decisive action.

In Cicero's case, the gap between his *popularis* rhetoric and his actions opened up abruptly when he forced Catilina into open revolt and then pursued him and his followers to the death. Many public figures, however, would never find themselves in such revealing

---

[18] Valerius Maximus includes an entire chapter (7.5) in his *Memorable Deeds and Sayings* on electoral defeats, many of which arise from *faux pas* in dealing with citizens. So, for example, Scipio Nasica (cos. 138) is alleged to have failed in his first attempt to be elected as curule aedile because he asked a voter, whose (calloused) hand he was shaking, whether he walked on his hands (7.5.2).

[19] Cicero, *On Behalf of Plancius* 64–6.

[20] Morstein-Marx (2004: 204–240).

circumstances, and in the absence of political difference, other clues were looked for in order to judge a man. Late Republican oratory is bristling with invective: not only are there substantial passages of invective in many of Cicero's speeches, but invective is also one aspect of oratory where we have access to some of his contemporaries' works.[21] Bold and scabrous criticism of political figures is prominent also in some of Catullus' poems. Recent work on invective has highlighted the links between the themes of invective and wider social norms.[22] Corbeill has argued that humorous invective in the late Republic relies on established and widespread beliefs about the relationship between appearance and character, for example, which underpin the concentration on appearance in Cicero's invective: people who look unattractive are also morally unworthy.[23]

Another approach to the function of invective is to relate it to the problem of individual identity. It is now not a matter for dispute that there were no political parties in the late Republic.[24] This absence of lasting organisational structures for political activity must be central to any understanding of Roman politics; and is crucially important in shaping the function of oratory. Without parties to command votes and distribute favours, aspirant politicians had to rely on other means to communicate a distinctive identity to their voters. Bribery was one of these, and complex networks developed to facilitate it.[25] The demonstrable importance of family was another: Romans voted for names they recognised, one might surmise, not only because of a conviction that ability was hereditary but simply because they did recognise the name. And opportunities to speak to the citizen body were potentially very important, and were consequently seized – by those who had confidence in their speaking abilities – when they arose. We have already observed the phenomenon of prosecutions being undertaken by very young men, as their first public appearance. Funeral speeches, too, offered the possibility of giving a speech outside the normal range of occasions, with their concomitant limits on who could speak; this, alongside the opportunity to retell one's

---

[21] Cicero's main invective targets are Verres (*Verrines*), Catilina (*Catilinarians*), Clodius (*On Behalf of Sestius*, *On Behalf of Milo*), Piso (*On the Consular Provinces*, *Against Piso*), Gabinius (*On the Consular Provinces*) and Antonius (*Philippics*). Paragraphs of invective also survive by other orators: most striking are those of Helvius Mancia (Valerius Maximus 6.2.8) and Marcus Caelius (Quintilian, *Education of the Orator* 4.2.123).

[22] Richlin (1992); Corbeill (1996); Krostenko (2001).

[23] Corbeill (1996: 14–56).

[24] Taylor (1949) remains a valuable study of the late Republic, despite its title; see further Brunt (1988: 443–502).

[25] Yakobson (1999: 26–43).

family history, made them attractive to the young politician. Caesar innovated by commemorating a female relative. The future emperor Tiberius delivered a funeral oration for his father at the age of nine; nothing is known of the content of the speech, though it is intriguing to speculate whether his recently acquired step-father Octavian – who was at precisely this time attempting to secure his position with the Roman aristocracy as he prepared for war with Antonius – had any hand in what he said.[26]

Invective can be seen as the converse of this straining for impact. A politician could supplement his positive self-portrayal with a demonstration that his rivals were not what they claimed to be. Oratory was one of the most effective ways of communicating the failings of others to the audiences which mattered: whether by the direct attack on another in the Senate or in front of the people, or more obliquely via the courts. And the traits which are attacked underscore the importance of appearance as well as behaviour in the creation of individual politicians' identities: Roman audiences were likely to be convinced by appeal to what they themselves had seen.

A good example of an invective encounter is the confrontation between Cicero and L. Calpurnius Piso during the 50s B.C. Cicero bore a deep grudge against him from the time of his being sent into exile during Piso's consulship in 58 B.C.: earlier, relations between the two men had been good and so Cicero regarded Piso's failure to stop Clodius as a personal betrayal.[27] On his return to Rome in 57 B.C. he pursued his enmity with Piso in a variety of speeches.[28] Initially these were delivered in Piso's absence, as the latter was proconsul in Macedonia after his consulship, and include Cicero's contribution to the senatorial debate in the early summer of 56 B.C. on choosing the consular provinces for the consuls who were about to be elected. Cicero argued in favour of designating Syria and Macedonia: this would inevitably mean the recall of both Piso and Gabinius. On Piso's return in 55 the two men clashed during a meeting of the Senate; Cicero wrote up his remarks as *Against Piso* and Piso responded with

---

[26] Suetonius, *Life of Tiberius* 6. Augustus himself had delivered the funeral oration for his grandmother at the age of twelve: Quintilian, *Education of the Orator* 12.6.1.; Suetonius, *Life of Augustus* 8.

[27] Cicero also expressed deep hostility towards Piso's consular colleague Gabinius; but he had not been close friends with Gabinius before his exile, and consequently the betrayal seems to have been less bitter.

[28] Cicero, *To the Senate after his Recall from Exile, To the Citizens after his Recall from Exile, On the Consular Provinces, Against Piso.*

his own written pamphlet.[29] Cicero's pursuit of Piso is an aspect of his attempt to re-establish himself after being exiled, and Piso's response, similarly, arises from the need to preserve face and refute the gross charges that Cicero laid against him.

Cicero's invective against Piso covers a huge range of topics, military as well as civilian. He has consistently failed to behave in a manner appropriate to a magistrate of the Roman people, and this includes not only his failures as a provincial governor but also a range of private behaviours: he drinks excessively, his hospitality is crude, he pretends to intellectual accomplishments but in practice is completely unable to understand the philosophical teaching of his friend Philodemus. And alongside serious charges about Piso's conduct is a deep concern with his appearance. Early in *Against Piso* Cicero says, 'It was not that servile complexion of yours, not your hairy cheeks, not your rotten teeth which deceived us: your eyes, your eyebrows, your forehead, your whole face – which is a kind of silent commentary on the mind – these drove men into error, these deceived those to whom you were not known and tricked and misled them.'[30] This passage is particularly revealing because it shows us Cicero both using the conventions of appearance-based invective and attempting to transcend them.[31] The problem which Piso poses for Cicero is that he does not look the part: Cicero is constantly accusing him of being a bad Roman and a bad magistrate, but Piso looks like an austere, upright Roman. Cicero therefore argues that there is a gap, in this case, between appearance and reality: the normal signs do not work. However, rather than allowing this to cast doubt on the entire system of drawing moral conclusions from men's appearances, Cicero instead uses this instance as further evidence of Piso's unreliability: he goes around projecting a deceptive appearance. And Cicero is also willing to draw attention to those unattractive aspects of Piso's appearances which do confirm his invective.

Oratory was a medium for attack; it could also itself be the subject of criticism. This is hardly surprising: given the importance of speaking among the things which politicians did, it provides an attractive focus for criticism. The performance and reception of oratory were matters for adult male citizens; speakers who did not securely

---

[29] Asconius 2C; Cicero, *Letters to his Brother Quintus* 3.1.11; Nisbet (1961: 199–202).

[30] *Against Piso* 1, *non enim nos color iste seruilis, non pilosae genae, non dentes putridi deceperunt: oculi supercilia frons uultus denique totus, qui sermo quidam tacitus mentis est, hic in fraudem homines impulit, hic eos quibus eras ignotus decepit fefellit induxit.*

[31] Corbeill (1996: 169–173).

demonstrate that they belonged to this group provided rich scope for hostile comment. Some areas which provoked anxiety can be traced in actual criticism of orators and oratory; the advice and warnings to be found in rhetorical handbooks and treatises gives further clues concerning behaviours which could leave the orator vulnerable.

The orator, according to the canons of rhetoric, had to be competent in five areas: finding arguments (*inuentio*), putting them in order (*dispositio*), memorising them (*memoria*), expressing them in the appropriate language (*elocutio*) and delivering them (*actio*). Of these five, delivery and style afforded the greatest scope for mistakes and for moral censure. Finding and arranging arguments were areas where greater or lesser competence could be displayed, and the handbooks are naturally concerned to convey good practice. Failures of memory were noted and skill admired.[32] But the richest scope for policing the orator lay in assessing how he used his voice and body when speaking and what language he used to express himself.

The connection which could be made between the language an individual uses and his putative moral character is made absolutely explicit in a letter of the younger Seneca.[33] He is responding to a query from Lucilius about the causes of corrupt style, and his answer is that style matches way of life, and so a corrupt way of life will be reflected in a corrupt style.[34] To illustrate his answer he takes Maecenas as an example: Maecenas' morals were corrupt and so was his style of speech. His clothes are too flowing; when he appeared in public he covered his head but left his ears showing; he frequently went through the marriage ceremony with his wife. And this 'softness' and eccentricity is reflected in the way he spoke: 'Was not his speech just as untrammelled as he himself was self-indulgent? Were his words not just as peculiar as his appearance, retinue, house and wife? . . . And so you'll see the tortuous, rambling, unrestrained style of a drunk.'[35] Underlying much of Seneca's stylistic advice in this letter is anxiety about the correct display of masculinity. He concludes the

---

[32] The elder Curio (cos. 76) had a particularly bad memory, according to Cicero (*Brutus* 217): 'So lacking was he in ability to remember that often when he had put forward three headings he would either add a fourth or forget the third' (*memoria autem ita fuit nulla, ut aliquotiens, tria cum proposuisset, aut quartum adderet aut tertium quaereret*; Hortensius, by contrast, was remarkable for his prowess in the skill (*Brutus* 310; a particular feat of his memory became exemplary: Seneca, *Controuersiae* 1 pr. 19; Quintilian, *Education of the Orator* 11.2.24).

[33] Seneca, *Letters* 114.

[34] Seneca, *Letters* 114.1, *talis hominibus fuit oratio qualis uita.*

[35] Seneca, *Letters* 114.4, *non oratio eius aeque soluta est quam ipse discinctus? non tam insignia illius uerba sunt quam cultus, quam comitatus, quam domus, quam uxor?... uidebis itaque eloquentiam ebrii hominis inuolutam et errantem et licentiae plenam.*

section on how best to speak by explaining to Lucilius that, providing his spirit is sound, his speech will be 'vigorous, strong and masculine'.[36] The fear about failing to project the correct masculine identity is pervasive in Roman discussions of how to speak in public, and has been the focus of a great deal of recent critical interest.[37] The details which were seized upon by Roman commentators and orators as potential betrayers of their masculine selves are interestingly revealing of the way in which masculinity was constructed; in general, one can note the extent to which oratory is a focus for the debate. Oratory was a place where the Roman elite was visible, and it was a place where its members articulated to one another and to the Roman state more widely what identity they did and should have.

Status was another area where inappropriate oratory could leave the speaker vulnerable to attack. One specific area of concern was the boundary between oratory and acting. There were significant points of similarity between the two activities: the effective use of gesture and voice was essential to both actor and orator, and both performed in front of large, unpredictable audiences.[38] Cicero draws an analogy with acting when he describes what a court looks and feels like when it is receiving a great oratorical performance, with the result that 'anyone who sees it from a distance – even if he doesn't know what case is being heard – nonetheless understands that the speaker is a success and that a Roscius is on the stage'.[39] Roscius, unquestionably the greatest actor of the late Republic, was a friend of Cicero and Hortensius; he also wrote a book in which he compared oratory and acting.[40] Cicero claims to have studied Roscius' delivery, as well as that of Aesopus, who specialised in tragic roles; but, according to Valerius Maximus, Roscius and Aesopus in turn studied Hortensius' gesture to improve their own acting.[41] There was a productive dialogue going on between practitioners at the highest levels of both activities.[42] Cicero draws on dramatic themes and characters in a number of his speeches and two in particular – *On Behalf of Quintus*

---

[36] Seneca, *Letters* 114.22, *robusta, fortis, uirilis*.

[37] See in particular Edwards (1993: 63–97); Gleason (1995); Gunderson (2000); Dugan (2005).

[38] Graf (1991).

[39] Cicero, *Brutus* 290, *qui haec procul uideat, etiam si quid agatur nesciat, at placere tamen et in scaena esse Roscium intellegat*.

[40] Macrobius, *Saturnalia* 3.14.12.

[41] Valerius Maximus 8.10.2.

[42] Quintilian (*Education of the Orator* 12.5.5) praises his contemporary Trachalus as 'better than any tragic actor that I ever heard' (*super omnis quos ego quidem audierim tragoedos*).

Roscius the Actor and *On Behalf of Marcus Caelius Rufus* – are very largely structured around dramatic motifs.[43] In *On the Orator*, Cicero draws on acting for a wide range of comparative material as he assesses the orator's role. But the references to acting in this work also indicate that the connection was a potential problem, at least for orators, inasmuch as he includes cautions about the importance of retaining a distinction between what actors and orators do. So, for example, in the discussion of humour in book 2, the aspiring orator is warned against provoking laughter in a manner which recalls mime-actors too closely.[44] In book 3, Crassus opens the section on gesture by saying:

Gesture should accompany all these emotions: not the kind of gesture used on the stage, which illustrates individual words, but one which indicates content and arguments as a whole, not through description but by implication. This type of gesture requires a strong masculine turn of the body which comes from handling weapons and even from the exercise-pitch rather than actors and the stage.[45]

The social status of actors was low, and their craft frivolous.[46] Orators needed to exercise care, not because there was any danger that they could literally be confused with actors but because inappropriate use of gestures and language which seemed too actorly could compromise their dignity and thus their effectiveness.

There was also considerable concern about professionalism, at least in relation to forensic oratory. On the one hand, there was a powerful and long-standing consensus among the elite that forensic oratory should not be one's full-time activity. Payment in cash to defence advocates in criminal cases, and those on both sides in civil cases was banned by the *lex Cincia* of 204 B.C., though the emperor Claudius relaxed the rule.[47] And this amateurism was underpinned by the myth that forensic advocacy was one of a number of protections which patrons provided for clients in return for their clients' services.[48] The reality was, naturally, rather different. The complexity of the orator's task meant that specialists were at an enormous advantage. In *On the Orator*, Crassus is made to criticise very sharply men who engaged in

---

[43] Geffcken (1973); Axer (1979).

[44] Cicero, *On the Orator* 2.239, 2.242, 2.275.

[45] Cicero, *On the Orator* 3.220, *omnis autem hos motus subsequi debet gestus, non hic uerba exprimens scaenicus sed uniuersam rem et sententiam non demonstratione, sed significatione declarans, laterum inflexione hac forti ac uirili, non ab scaena et histrionibus, sed ab armis aut etiam a palaestra.*

[46] Roscius, who achieved equestrian status and financial success, was a notable exception.

[47] Crook (1995: 129–131).

[48] On the responsibilities of the *patronus*, see David (1992: 49–211).

forensic advocacy without an adequate knowledge of civil law.[49] And it is absolutely obvious from Cicero's own forensic career, as well as his *Brutus*, that there were men who specialised in forensic oratory.[50] Moreover, even though direct payment was not permitted, being defended brought with it a set of obligations and there were a variety of ways in which those obligations could be discharged.[51]

Defence advocacy, even if undertaken regularly and in defence of persons whose links with their advocate came about only as a result of their trial, could therefore be rendered acceptable within aristocratic society relatively easily. Prosecution, however, was much more troubling. Given that prosecutions were a matter of private enterprise, the man bringing the charge could not hide behind an anonymised state. It is true that the praetor had to accept the charge in order for the case to proceed to trial; but it would nonetheless be apparent to all that, in most cases, the very existence of a charge depended upon the action of a particular individual. Prosecutors were thus very liable to the accusation of cruelty and, given the rewards which followed successful prosecution, greed and profiteering.[52] When Cicero prosecuted Verres he took a great deal of care to present his action as a defence of the Sicilians from the predations of their former governor.[53] When he considered the ethics of prosecution much later in *On Duties* he argued that a single prosecution could be regarded as legitimate, especially given the benefit that could follow for the state, but habitual prosecution was not acceptable.[54] Savage penalties were laid down for those who undertook mischievous prosecutions.[55] And yet there clearly were men who made their living by undertaking prosecutions. Examples can be found in Cicero's opponents in some of his early speeches: Erucius in *On Behalf of Sextus Roscius* appears to be in this category. But in the Republican period this is a shadowy group: the object of ridicule and hostility in Cicero's oratory, whose bias obscures their identity and activities. In the Empire, prosecutors emerge with greater clarity and with an expanded role which arises

---

[49] Cicero, *On the Orator* 1.166–197.

[50] Burnand (2004).

[51] So, for example, Quintus Cicero regards Cicero's oratory, particularly his forensic oratory, as absolutely central to his bid for the consulship (Quintus Cicero, *Handbook of Electioneering* 2–6).

[52] Epstein (1987).

[53] Vasaly (1993: 205–217).

[54] Cicero, *On Duties* 2.49–51.

[55] In theory, at least, a prosecutor found guilty of *calumnia* lost his civil rights and was branded on the forehead with a K: see David (1992: 101–115).

from the emperor's concerns about treason; and, in elite writings, become a symbol of the faults of the political system as a whole.[56]

At a more fundamental level, oratorical performance could expose vulnerabilities in Roman identity. The development of oratory as a discipline and skill at Rome was marked by initial ambivalence towards its Greek origins and a shaky grasp of a distinct Roman identity was a weakness liable to criticism.[57] Cicero, who was not from Rome but Arpinum, was described by Catilina – according to Sallust – as a 'squatter in the city of Rome' and by Torquatus, his opponent in a forensic case held in 62 B.C., as a 'foreign tyrant'.[58] But oratory also provided opportunities to exploit Roman history. Torquatus, in the passage just discussed, apparently referred to the kings Numa and Tarquinius in order to set Cicero up as another absolute ruler from outside Rome. Cicero himself used examples drawn from Roman history with great frequency in his speeches,[59] including references which are grounded in the physical setting of his oratory.[60] So, for example, in his speech *On Behalf of Scaurus* from 54 B.C., he draws his audience's attention to the monuments which they can see around the Roman Forum which are connected with Scaurus' distinguished ancestors and relatives.[61] Through the use of shared history, articulated through familiar stories, Roman orators can appeal to their audience by constructing them as a privileged and exclusive group.[62]

Many of the concerns examined in this chapter came together in a vigorous set of exchanges about oratorical style from the 50s and 40s B.C. which set 'Atticism' against 'Asianism'.[63] Cicero was accused by some younger orators of Asianism, which seems to have meant an

[56] Rutledge (1999); Rivière (2002); and compare the importance of informers in Tacitus' *Annals*.

[57] I return to the origins of Roman rhetoric in the final chapter; on the links between Roman identity and language, see Hall (1998); Farrell (2001).

[58] Sallust, *Cat.* 31.7, *inquilinus ciuis urbis Romae*; Cicero, *On Behalf of Sulla* 22, *me tertium peregrinum regem esse dixisti*; Berry (1996: 182).

[59] Fleck (1993).

[60] Vasaly (1993).

[61] Vasaly (1993: 37–38).

[62] Gaius Fannius (cos. 122) made what was apparently an extraordinarily effective use of the appeal to an exclusive Roman identity in a speech he delivered in the year of his consulship in opposition to Gaius Gracchus' attempt to extend full citizenship to the Latins: 'I believe you think, if you give citizenship to the Latins, that you will continue to have room, as you do now, at public meetings and be able to participate in games and holidays. Surely you realise that they will take up all the spaces?' (Julius Victor 6.4 [Halm p. 402], *si Latinis ciuitatem dederitis, credo existimatis uos ita ut nunc constitistis in contione habituros locum aut ludis et festis diebus interfuturos. nonne illos omnia occupaturos putatis?*) On the extent of historical knowledge among Roman citizens generally, see Morstein-Marx (2004: 68–118).

[63] Wisse (1995).

excessively florid and bombastic style of speaking. His opponents, most prominently C. Licinius Calvus, claimed to display the virtues of Atticism, as manifested primarily in the orator Lysias: lucidity, simplicity and restraint. One of the major difficulties in assessing what exactly was at stake here is that the earliest surviving evidence comes only from Cicero's own *Brutus* and *Orator*, from 46 B.C., by which time Calvus himself was dead.[64] Cicero's approach to the problem is primarily to concentrate on the definition of Atticism and argue that, properly understood, this term includes a much wider range of style than the Roman Atticists allow. Demosthenes, and the grand style, are as integral to the Athenian achievement as Lysias: and once this is established, then Cicero's own range and power can themselves be seen as Attic.[65] In *Brutus*, indeed, Asianism is something which Cicero's great rival Hortensius displayed and not a label that Cicero applies to himself; Hortensius, too, was dead at the time of writing.[66] It is difficult not to think that Cicero is taking advantage of the demise of his rivals to close off this particular debate on style in a way which secures his lasting reputation. In particular, the surviving material on Calvus' oratory does not seem entirely to fit with Cicero's view of Atticism: neither the surviving fragments nor anecdotes about his performance suggest notable meagreness. Indeed, the elder Seneca remarks on Calvus as an orator with notably vehement delivery, so much so that during his prosecution of Vatinius, Vatinius was moved to say the jurors, 'Am I to be condemned, gentlemen of the jury, just because he is eloquent?'.[67] But however murky the details, some general observations can be made about the episode. It shows the extent to which stylistic discussion of oratory at Rome depended on an interpretative framework derived from Greece, a theme to which I return in the final chapter. There is a suggestion that morality is at stake in stylistic choices: in particular, 'Attic' oratory displays healthfulness, *sanitas*, and Asianism brings with it a suggestion of effeminacy.[68] And perhaps most striking is the relentless competitiveness between orators and their striving to gain advantage.

[64] There was a correspondence on stylistic matters between Cicero, Calvus and Brutus (Tacitus, *Dialogus* 18.5) but it does not survive.

[65] On Cicero's relationship more generally with the figure of Demosthenes as an oratorical model, see Wooten (1983)

[66] *Brutus* 325–327.

[67] Seneca, *Controuersiae* 7.4.6: *rogo uos, iudices, num, si iste disertus est, ideo me damnari oportet?*

[68] *Brutus* 278; compare Quintilian *I.O.* 12.10.15, where he records the accusation against Cicero, in the context of his alleged Asianism, that he was 'almost softer than a man should be' (*paene ... uiro molliorem*) in how he put words together.

The Roman orator had a difficult job. The value of his task was not in question. But relying on technical aids to improve his skills could always be met by the spectre of the elder Cato with his suggestion that the true Roman speaker was brief and simple, or – as Cicero found – the charge of Asianism, with its suggestion of excess and effeminacy.[69] The elite orator needed always to avoid charges of professionalism and of profiteering. And for those practising in the imperial period there was the constant fear that oratory was now condemned to futility and irrelevance; the art had received its highest expression in Cicero's achievements and political change made it impossible for anyone to surpass him.

Cicero himself can be seen as one of the originators of this view, in his pessimistic account of contemporary oratory in *Brutus*. And I shall conclude this chapter by considering his extraordinary reprieve as an orator, after the composition of *Brutus*, in the year following Caesar's assassination. In the *Philippics*, the figure of the orator is one of the subjects which Cicero uses to attack Antonius and defend his own actions; and in Cicero's posthumous reputation this set of speeches becomes emblematic both of Cicero's personal brilliance and of the place of oratory in Roman life, as well as marking a decisive point at which the speaking orator is overtaken by the written text.[70] In these speeches, Antonius is portrayed – with the partial exception only of the first – as an enemy of the Roman state in the broadest possible terms. Within this characterisation, his lack of ability as an orator is prominent, particularly in the second speech. The *Second Philippic* falls into two parts: in the first (3–41) Cicero defends himself against the charges which Antonius had brought against him at the meeting of the Senate on 19 September, which Cicero did not attend. The second part (44–114) contains the attack by Cicero on Antonius. Judging by Cicero's response, Antonius' attack covered Cicero's public life from the time of the Catilinarian conspiracy onwards and Cicero starts from Antonius' childhood.[71] His description of Antonius as an orator comes between the two sections of the speech and enables him to round off his refutation of the substance of Antonius' attack with criticism of his skill in delivering the attack in a speech.

---

[69] A separate argument – not to be attempted here – could link fear of oratorical excess with wider fears about luxury and consumption.

[70] Butler (2002).

[71] Cicero, *Second Philippic* 2.44, 'Do you want me to consider you from childhood? I think you do; let's begin at the beginning' (*Visne igitur te inspiciamus a puero? Sic opinor; a principio ordiamur*)

'Was it to collect this material, you fool, that you spent so many days declaiming in a borrowed villa? But then, as your friends keep saying, you declaim in order to get wine out of your system rather than to sharpen your wits.'[72] Cicero then compares the results of Antonius' futile practice with his drunken colleagues with the achievement as an orator of his grandfather, another Marcus Antonius and one of the greatest orators of his generation.[73] The context of the speech can explain, in part, Cicero's decision to make oratory one aspect of the struggle between himself and Antonius, given that he had just been the objective of a very sustained and public attack from Antonius. Cicero was already at a very considerable disadvantage in this contest because he did not dare respond orally to Antonius' attack but was compelled instead to write it. The extraordinary success of this ploy in the subsequent history of Cicero's works can obscure the frustration which Cicero must have felt in not having the opportunity to speak to the Senate in his own defence. So demonstrating that Antonius was an incompetent orator who relied on other people's words was rather important if Cicero were to maintain authority in the developing struggle. However, a further valuable consequence of this tactical decision is to emphasise that oratory is at the heart of what divides Cicero from Antonius. On this presentation, oratory is one of the aspects of the *res publica* which Antonius seeks to destroy through his ignorance and incompetence. One sign of Cicero's success in his attack on Antonius' oratory is that Antonius himself is seldom regarded as a competent orator, despite the fact that he spoke with success on a number of well-documented occasions, including as one of the prosecutors of Milo in 52 B.C., and produced written versions of some of his speeches.[74]

Butler has shown how Cicero's use of writing, and of written evidence, affected profoundly his posthumous reputation and reception. It was through the *Philippics*, above all, that Cicero came to be one of the symbolic defenders of Republican freedom.[75] His legacy was debated in the historiography of the Augustan period but the positive interpretation became a staple of declamation and exemplary

---

[72] Cicero, *Second Philippic* 2.42, *haec ut conligeres, homo amentissime, tot dies in aliena uilla declamasti? quamquam tu quidem, ut tui familiarissimi dictitant, uini exhalandi, non ingeni acuendi causa declamas.*

[73] This M. Antonius (cos. 99 B.C.) was one of the two main speakers in Cicero's *On the Orator*; the other was L. Crassus (cos. 95 B.C.); see Fantham (2004: 26–48).

[74] For details of Antonius' oratory, see Malcovati (1976: no. 159); David (1992: 854–855).

[75] Richlin (1999).

literature.[76] But writing matters in Cicero's case because it offers a simulacrum of oral performance. His actions continued to resonate with his imperial readers because his writings allowed them to play out, over and over again, the orator standing up and speaking in defence of the Republic. The *Philippics* offer a defence of freedom and a promise of self-sacrifice whose emotional resonance is compelling. But they exercise a profound effect in part because we, as readers, can follow the story over time, from September 44 to April 43, filling in as we go everything which Cicero could not yet know and which contributed to his assassination. His fate is set up and charted over thirteen identifiable occasions on which he addressed Senate or people with words which are still available.[77] And, through the combination of his skill, the circumstances of his death, and the political transformation which was going on at that time, Cicero became the exemplary orator of Rome.

I have considered in this chapter a range of pressure points in oratorical identity, and the ways in which acute orators exploited them to attack their rivals and to protect themselves. In the final chapter I approach the question of the orator's identity from a different angle: the methods by which young men were turned into orators.

[76] Pierini (2003: 3–54).
[77] Steel (2005: 140–146).

IV THE ORATOR'S EDUCATION

The order of chapters in this book may seem paradoxical: the finished orator is considered before the processes by which he reached that state are examined. The order is indeed back-to-front from the perspective of an individual orator's trajectory, whose training must inevitably precede his activity. But in the wider context of an attempt to understand the nature of oratorical training in the Roman world it makes sense to move from the practising orator back to the embryonic form, since the expectations and norms imposed on the fully fledged orator are the foundations which support the system of oratorical education. This observation does not imply any necessary confidence that Roman oratorical education was designed for the creation of orators who met the criteria for and defused the anxieties about oratory which I discussed in the previous chapter. And even if the material which a modern audience can access did suggest that Roman oratorical education was indeed good at producing Roman orators, there is of course no guarantee that actual practice in classrooms across the Empire bore any relation to these writings or displayed any competence at its task. But an awareness of the practice of oratory can usefully inform analysis of how orators were trained.

The earlier chapters of this book have considered oratory as a set of occasions when men spoke in front of an audience. I have been concerned primarily with oratory in its 'live', performed state; the written texts which provide us with our most significant means of accessing Roman oratory are a product of that performance environment and derive much of their importance from it. The occasions when written speeches do not have spoken originals serve to confirm this: without the possibility of spoken performance the texts of Cicero's *Verrines*, or *Second Philippic*, become pointless, even though these particular speeches were never actually delivered. It was only because they might have been delivered that there was any point to Cicero's having versions disseminated as though they had. However, once one begins to consider the means by which aspirant young men became orators the focus shifts from the occasions of performance to a variety of simulacra of the orator's task.[1]

---

[1] The texts of speeches may themselves be regarded as such: Cicero certainly was conscious of the value of his writings as models for aspirant young orators, even if this was not the chief motive in his writing them (but cf. Stroh 1975).

However, before turning to the education of orators two issues need to be discussed briefly. One is the difference between oratory and rhetoric, which, for the purposes of this chapter, can be understood in terms of practice and theory. Oratory refers, first, to speeches delivered orally in the variety of situations discussed in Chapter 1 and then, by extension, to the texts which purport to record these words. Rhetoric, by contrast, is the name for the techniques through which people might speak more effectively. So an orator need know nothing of rhetoric, and a rhetorician may never have delivered a piece of oratory; in practice, however, at Rome, orators sought to benefit from rhetoric as much as they could, and rhetoricians were conscious that their pupils were potential orators. And some orators, most notably Cicero and Tacitus, also wrote works on rhetoric.[2]

The second issue is the place of rhetorical education within Roman education more generally.[3] Rhetoric was one of the more advanced subjects: those studying it would be restricted to the minuscule proportion of Romans who had more than a few years' education.[4] It also had a distinct position within the topics of Roman education, inasmuch as it alone had the potential to lead into practical activity. I have discussed in Chapter 3 the ways in which the practice of oratory as a constant and lucrative occupation could be regarded with disapproval. In educational terms, there were no qualifications which could certify an individual's competence: orators demonstrated their ability only when they spoke.

As soon as one begins to consider the nature of oratorical education at Rome, it becomes clear that there were two methods which were regarded as being fundamentally different: practical experience through the shadowing of an established figure on the one hand, and on the other rhetorical education within a school environment. This opposition is presented with striking clarity in Tacitus' *Dialogus* (34–35). Messalla, the speaker, has described the range of education which orators used to get (28–32) in order to explain the decline in standards of oratory at Rome and has now moved on to considering the kinds of practical training young orators get. He gives a stark contrast between the past and the present day:

---

[2] Cicero, *On Invention, On the Orator, Orator, Brutus, On the Best Kind of Orator, Topica, Paradoxes of the Stoics*; Tacitus, *Dialogus*. Rhetoricians in antiquity did not confine their critical responses to oratory; see Laird (1999: 6–7).

[3] Marrou (1956); Bonner (1977); Morgan (1998a).

[4] Harris (1989).

In earlier generations the young man who was preparing for a civilian career . . . was taken by his father or by a relative to whichever orator was then pre-eminent in the state. He would become accustomed to follow him around, escort him, attend all his forensic and contional speeches . . . but now our young men are taken to the schools of the men who are called *rhetors* . . . and there I could not say what does more harm to their talents, the place itself or their fellow pupils or the nature of their studies.[5]

The *Dialogus* is a work concerned with the processes of historical and political change and the effects of those changes on the practice and quality of oratory.[6] In this context, Messalla's very broad generalisation should be treated with a degree of caution, as well as an indication of the close connection between education and practice. Nonetheless, Cicero's career provides us with examples of how this practical apprenticeship actually worked: indeed, Messalla refers to Cicero's account of his own education in *Brutus* a little earlier in the *Dialogus*. In this passage of *Brutus* (304–323) Cicero describes his own formation as an orator up to the outbreak of the civil war. There is a variety of different elements in his training. Part of it is indeed attendance on his elders, such as Messalla describes: so he learnt civil law with Scaevola and paid great attention to Sulpicius' *contiones* during the latter's tribunate (306). Elsewhere Cicero describes how he spent time with Crassus and Antonius as a boy (*On the Orator* 2.3). In *Brutus*, too, Cicero refers to his own direct experience of the two men's oratory. Another element which Cicero picks out is practice on his own or with his contemporaries: and for this he uses the verb *declamito*, though with an apology for using a neologism (*Brutus* 310). A third major training activity was study of philosophy: first in Rome, with the Stoic Diodotus, where he concentrated particularly on dialectic, and then at Athens with the Academic philosopher Antiochus.[7]

This amalgamation of practical training with broad cultural expertise is seized upon by the speakers in the *Dialogus* as a single and unproblematic approach to becoming an orator which can be contrasted with the pernickety and artificial exercises to be found in the rhetorical schools. But it is a synthesis not without its own internal tensions, and is itself very much a creation of Cicero. A consideration

---

[5] Tacitus, *Dialogus* 34–35, *ergo apud maiores nostros iuuenis ille qui foro et eloquentiae parabatur … deducebatur a patre uel a propinquis ad eum oratorem qui principem in ciuitate locum obtinebat. hunc sectari, hunc prosequi, huius omnibus dictionibus interesse siue in iudiciis siue in contionibus assuescebat … at nunc adulescentuli nostri deducuntur in scholas istorum qui rhetores uocantur …: in quibus non facile dixerim utrumne locus ipse an condiscipuli an genus studiorum plus mali ingeniis afferant.*

[6] Mayer (2001: 16–47).

[7] Rawson (1983: 12–28).

of the different elements which go into the mixture throws some light on the ways in which oratorical education developed at Rome and the conflicting claims which it addressed.

One fundamental tension is between Greece and Rome. Oratory itself was regarded as part of Roman political life since the foundation of the Republic; but rhetoric was an import from Greece. Its arrival was placed in the earlier part of the second century B.C.: the precise details of its acclimatisation at Rome are not recoverable, but rhetoric was clearly located within a variety of practices which were seen to have arrived in Rome as a direct, and deleterious, consequence of the defeat of the Macedonian kingdom and the later absorption of western Asia Minor into Rome's sphere of influence. Indeed, one of the reasons why it is so difficult to give an account of the development of rhetoric at Rome is that a few key episodes become exemplary in a narrative of moral decline and the corruption of Roman character.

At the heart of our knowledge of this complex picture is the elder Cato.[8] We have already seen him as the first Roman orator to exploit the possibilities of writing. In his public life he promulgated a sternly virtuous line which can be seen on occasion to apply specifically to public speaking. Indeed, his maxims on public speaking can be interpreted in the context of the development of rhetoric as a skill and as a reaction to aspects of this development. According to a late rhetorician, Cato encapsulated his advice on oratory in the words *rem tene, uerba sequentur*.[9] This could be seen as an exhortation to simplicity in the face of instruction which complicated the act of speaking through the introduction of rules for organising material and embellishing language. Cato's maxim, by contrast, insists on the primacy of the mastery of content, from which appropriate language will automatically follow.

Cato also described the orator as *uir bonus dicendi peritus*:[10] this emphasis on moral virtue as the leading characteristic of the orator had a long afterlife in Roman reflection on rhetoric, and can be related to the longstanding debate between philosophy and rhetoric in Greek thought, to which I return below. In this context, Cato can be seen as rejecting the artifice of rhetoric, with its promise of persuasive speech regardless of the moral value of the case argued. If, however, the chief qualification of the orator is his moral worth, then

---

[8] Astin (1978: 131–156); Gruen (1992: 52–83).
[9] 'Hold onto the subject, the words will follow'; Julius Victor 374 (Halm).
[10] Seneca, *Controuersia* 1 pr. 9; Quintilian, *Education of the Orator* 12.1.1.

anxieties about using rhetoric in order to promote injustice cannot arise.[11]

An anecdote involving the elder Cato reveals his hostility to rhetoric more directly than his comments on the orator and oratory. In 155 a diplomatic embassy containing three distinguished philosophers came from Athens to Rome to ask for help in an internal dispute between Athens and Oropus: the matter had gone to arbitration with Sicyon, which had found against Athens, and the Athenians wanted Roman support in being let off the subsequent hefty fine. The philosophers were Critolaus, a Peripatetic, Diogenes, a Stoic, and Carneades, an Academic philosopher. While they were waiting to address the Senate they gave a series of public lectures which were extremely popular with young Romans. Cato was disturbed by their success and consequently urged the Senate to hear their case, and reach a decision, as soon as possible, so that the ambassadors could leave Rome.[12] According to Plutarch, Cato's fear was that young Romans might be seduced by the eloquence of the Athenian philosophers into attempting to base their reputations on oratory rather than fighting; and Plutarch offers what purports to be a quotation from Cato's actual speech to the Senate, 'We ought to investigate and make up our minds about the embassy as soon as possible, so that the envoys may return to their studies and lecture to Greek young men whilst Roman youth pay attention to the laws and magistrates, as before'.[13]

This anecdote portrays the elder Cato as a man who was deeply suspicious of Greek culture, particularly because of its potential effects on Romans; and this presentation dominates much of the biographical tradition about him. But he had considerable knowledge of what he feared: his writings, in particular, display a familiarity with Greek culture and in certain cases reminiscence of a passage in a Greek model seems highly plausible.[14] Cato's overall position on oratory and rhetoric needs, therefore, to be assessed with considerable care. Direct use of the techniques of Greek rhetoric cannot be

---

[11] Seneca, however, seems to have regarded *uir* as the crucial word: he continues after the quotation, 'Go now and look for orators among the smooth plucked men of today, men only in their lusts'; see above, Chapter 3.

[12] Gellius, *Attic Nights* 6.14.8–10; Plutarch, *Cato the Elder* 22–23.

[13] Plutarch, *Cato the Elder* 22.5, δεῖν οὖν τὴν ταχίστην γνῶναι τι καὶ ψηφίσασθαι περὶ τῆς πρεσβείας, ὅπως οὗτοι μὲν λἐπὶ τὰς σχολὰς τραπόμενοι διαλέγωνται παισὶν Ἑλλήνων, οἱ δὲ Ῥωμαίων νέοι τῶν νόμων καὶ τῶν ἀρχόντων ὡς πρότερον ἀκούωσι. This speech is not recorded in Malcovati.

[14] Examples are gathered by Gruen (1992: 57–8).

documented and there is little evidence that he wrote systematically on rhetoric.[15] Of the two observations on speaking discussed above, *uir bonus dicendi peritus* is attested to have come from the book of advice he wrote for his son, and this work, *ad Filium*, is a plausible source for the other, too. And if this is correct, we have here pithy summations of an approach – possibly designed to be learned by heart – and not a detailed or nuanced treatment of the subject of rhetoric. Nonetheless, it is possible to extract a consistent picture from them. They can be seen as the embodiment of what might be described as an anti-theoretical approach to the activity of speaking, indeed, perhaps, an anti-rhetorical one: a knowledge of the subject in question and an appropriate moral disposition are all that is required to speak effectively. This is a very different approach from one which simply ignores the question of how to attain oratorical competence: Cato seems to have decided that rhetoric could not simply be disregarded.

It is hardly surprising that Romans responded with enthusiasm to polished speech when they were exposed to it. As we have seen, ability as a public speaker was so important a skill for the elite that anything which offered the possibility of improvement was likely to find a ready market. And in the desire to speak well Romans seem to have ignored some aspects of the Greek intellectual milieu which they were absorbing. One of the things which is curious about the anecdote about Carneades is a blurring of the distinction between philosophy and rhetoric. Carneades and his colleagues were philosophers, not rhetoricians. But – according to Plutarch's version – what attracted young Romans to their lectures was the desire to learn how to speak well as much as the desire to learn about philosophy. Naturally, as ambassadors representing their community at Rome, they would be effective speakers: that would have been one of the criteria behind their selection. It was not foolish of the Romans to be impressed by their abilities to speak in public. But in turning to philosophers for instruction in rhetoric, the aspirant Romans of the mid-second century were, perhaps unwittingly, ignoring the major cultural dispute between the two disciplines which went back at least as far as Plato's writings. Philosophers and rhetoricians had been in competition since that time to establish their own discipline as the universal method for understanding the world and men's actions within it; and central to

---

[15] Astin (1978: 131–156).

the philosophical attack on rhetoric was the argument that rhetorical skill, divorced from moral understanding, was a lethal tool.[16]

Cato's description of the orator suggests that he at least was aware of the difficulties which could follow from removing moral content from the orator's task. Insofar as the evidence allows us to speculate, however, this debate was not a cause of major concern as rhetoric developed at Rome. On the one hand, as in the case of the Athenian embassy, little clear distinction is drawn between different manifestations of Greek intellectual prowess which were consumed eagerly and criticised heavily.[17] On the other, the moral probity of rhetoric is assured through its manifestation as an essential part of a civilised state.

This view is articulated with striking clarity and assurance in the preface to the first book of Cicero's *On Invention*, which may be the earliest surviving rhetoric handbook in Latin. The passage is worth quoting in full:

I have frequently asked myself whether facility in speaking and great devotion to eloquence have brought more good or evil to men and communities. When I consider the troubles in our state, and reflect upon past calamities in outstanding cities, I understand that not the least part of their troubles was generated by persuasive men. But when, on the other hand, I begin to study in the written record events remote in time from our own period, I see many cities founded, very many wars brought to a close, and lasting alliances and the most sacred of friendships have been established through the operation of reason but more easily too through eloquence. And reason itself has led me, as I reflected at length, to the opinion, above all, that whilst wisdom without eloquence can do little good to communities, eloquence without wisdom is very frequently a source of harm and can never be beneficial. And so anyone who spends their time and effort exclusively in the practice of oratory, neglecting the study of honourable and upright behaviour, is turned into a citizen who is useless to himself and dangerous for his country; but the man who arms himself with eloquence, not so as to act against the advantage of his country but to be able to defend it, seems to me to be a man and a citizen who will be most useful and supportive of both his friends' interests and those of his community.[18]

---

[16] Vickers (1988: 148–178).

[17] Rawson (1985); Gruen (1992).

[18] *On Invention* 1.1, *saepe et multum hoc mecum cogitaui, bonine an mali plus attulerit hominibus et ciuitatibus copia dicendi ac summum eloquentiae studium. nam cum et nostrae rei publicae detrimenta considero et maximarum ciuitatum ueteres animo calamitates colligo, non minimam uideo per disertissimos homines inuectam partem incommodorum; cum autem res ab nostra memoria propter uetustatem remotas ex litterarum monumentis repetere instituo, multas urbes constitutas, plurima bella restincta, firmissimas societates, sanctissimas amicitias intellego cum animi ratione tum facilius eloquentia comparatas. ac me quidem diu cogitantem ratio ipsa in hanc potissimum sententiam ducit, ut existimem sapientiam sine eloquentia parum prodesse ciuitatibus, eloquentiam uero sine sapientia nimium obesse plerumque, prodesse nunquam. quare si quis omissis rectissimis atque honestissimis studiis rationis et offici consumit omnem operam in exercitatione dicendi, is inutilis sibi, perniciosus patriae ciuis*

Cicero develops this idea over a further four chapters, which offer an account of the development of oratory and its relationship to the establishment of human communities, followed by reflections on how eloquence subsequently became a force for evil.[19] As an opening to an instructional manual, these reflections provide a bold acknowledgement that what is being offered in the work to come has its own dangers: and this starting point is not without persuasive force, since the reader can have confidence that his guide has thought extensively about the issues involved in this skill. But the problem of the misuse of oratory is not lasting. By the end of these opening chapters, it has been resolved: it is precisely because oratory has the capacity to be misused by 'the stupid and unprincipled' that it should be studied so that effective opposition can be offered to such men.[20] There is no real attempt in this work to resolve the issues which arise from the amorality of rhetoric.

However inconclusive and superficial the theoretical observations at the opening of the *On Invention* they do nonetheless indicate that such debates were now part of the Roman experience of rhetoric. More generally, *On Invention* gives us a sense of what rhetorical education at Rome in the 90s and 80s was like. The opening of the first book is not typical of the whole text: along with the opening chapters of the second book, it is among the few places in the work which break free from the narrow concerns of a technical manual. Much of the content of *On Invention* is remarkably similar to the section on invention in the anonymous treatise on rhetoric, *ad Herennium*. The precise relationship between these two works, and their relative dating, is impossible to determine.[21] But it is certain that both authors are drawing on the rhetorical theory of Hermagoras: both use Hermagoras' status-theory as the means of determining the point at issue in forensic cases and show very considerable similarities in the ordering of the material on the finding of arguments. The most likely intermediary is a teacher of rhetoric active in Rome, whom both authors attended during the 90s B.C.; and then soon afterwards they amplified and embellished their notes into treatises, though in Cicero's case he appears to have lost interest in the project, or been otherwise distracted, as his book covers only one out of the five parts of oratory. The *ad Herennium*, however, deals with all five parts.

alitur; qui uero ita sese armat eloquentia, ut non oppugnare commoda patriae, sed pro his propugnare possit, is mihi uir et suis et publicis rationibus utilissimus atque amicissimus ciuis fore uidetur.

[19] On ancient accounts of the origins of human civilisation see Campbell (2003: 9–18).
[20] *On Invention* 1.5.
[21] Corbeill (2002: 31–47).

The existence of these works confirms that education from professionals existed alongside practical training in the company of senior Romans: the aspirant Roman made use of both sources of information and improvement. But they also indicate some kind of market for written instruction in Latin on rhetoric: a market that was new, or at least had hitherto not been fully catered for.[22] We cannot be sure why either author wrote down his notes in systematic form, or how widely they envisaged their work circulating. But in Cicero's case it is at least possible that he wanted wide circulation and was using it as a way of getting his name known as someone with ability as a speaker.[23] This in turn would suggest that by the 90s B.C. Rome was an environment in which demonstrable rhetorical competence was an asset.

Finally, these two works contribute to our understanding of the complexity of the relationship between oratory at Rome and its Greek theoretical base. Whatever suspicion may have been felt in the earlier part of the second century B.C., by some Romans at least, about Greek influence over the teaching of oratory at Rome had dissipated to the extent that Greek was regarded by some as the only language suitable for rhetorical instruction. In 92 B.C. the censors, L. Licinius Crassus and Cn. Domitius Ahenobarbus, expressed strong disapprobation of the existence in Rome of schools which offered oratorical training in Latin. Suetonius preserves the text of their decree in his book *On Grammarians and Rhetors*:

We have been informed that there exist men who have set up a new sort of teaching and that young men gather at their school; they call themselves 'Latin rhetors' and there young men waste away entire days. Our ancestors established what they wanted their children to learn and what sorts of schools they wished them to attend: these novelties, which are against established practice and the habits of our ancestors, are not pleasing and do not seem right. Therefore it seems good to us to make our opinion clear both to those who keep these schools and those who frequent them: we do not approve.[24]

---

[22] As discussed above, there is considerable doubt as to whether Cato the elder ever wrote a work on rhetoric. M. Antonius (cos. 99) wrote a work on oratory, but it was insubstantial – it is described as a *libellus* – and apparently circulated without his knowledge: Cicero, *On the Orator* 1.94, 1.208; Quintilian, *Education of the Orator* 3.1.19.

[23] Steel (2005).

[24] Suetonius, *On Grammarians and Rhetors* 25.2; Gellius, *Attic Nights* 15.11.2, *renuntiatum est nobis esse homines qui nouum genus disciplinae instituerunt, ad quos iuuentus in ludum conueniat; eos sibi nomen imposuisse Latinos rhetorias, ibi homines adulescentulos dies totos desidere. maiores nostri quae liberos suos discere et quos in ludos itare uellent instituerunt; haec noua, quae practer consuetudinem ac morem maiorum fiunt, neque placent neque recta uidentur. qua propter et iis qui eos ludos habent et iis qui eo uenire consuerunt uisum est faciundum ut ostenderemus nostram sententiam: nobis non placere.*

It is very unclear why the censors took this step.[25] Some interpreters have seen this as a simply a pedagogical matter: the censors were taking the view that the instruction on offer in these schools – and it is not known how many might have fallen into this category – was not of an adequate standard. This is certainly the line which Cicero adopts in the passing reference to the controversy which he has Crassus make in *On the Orator*: there was nothing of pedagogical value in these schools.[26] However, many have felt that the involvement of the censors in this matter must have been due to some political ramification, and most who adopt this line see the closure of the schools in 92 B.C. in connection with the outbreak of the Social War only a year later. These Latin schools would then be an element in Italian desire for political representation in Rome, offering a means by which men who aspired to gain recognition for their communities could acquire the skills necessary for such an enterprise; and it is possible too that they had distinct links with politicians who supported a radically *popularis* line.

The evidence is, however, too partial to sustain such an interpretation securely; and it may depend on assumptions about access to Greek culture throughout the Italian peninsula which are not sustainable. But this episode does demonstrate that the act of teaching oratory was, at Rome, inherently political because of the vital importance in the political process of being able to speak well. There need have been no specific anxiety about the identity of those who frequented the Latin schools, or indeed about those who ran them, for the censors to believe that there existence was contrary to the existence of the state. That, indeed, was all that their edict meant; and the schools do not seem to have closed. What can securely be drawn from this episode is both the fact that rhetorical education was a matter with which the highest magistrates could legitimately concern themselves and that the transformation in the intellectual scene at Rome over the half century since Cato the Elder had led to Greek being the undisputed medium for this aspect of elite education and the correspondingly inferior status of Latin. Indeed, from this perspective, the decision of both Cicero and the anonymous author of the *ad Herennium* to write technical works about rhetoric in Latin cannot be an entirely neutral contribution to the debate. These works transmit into Latin a technical vocabulary for the analysis of rhetoric:

[25] On the episode, see Gruen (1990: 179–191); Kaster (1995: 273–275) .
[26] Cicero, *On the Orator* 3.93–95.

the similarities between the works suggest that a single teacher may be behind many choices of terminology, but some divergences indicate that the two authors may also have taken a hand in creating the language to match the resources of Greek.

Much later in his career Cicero returned to writing about oratory and in his mature works he demonstrates an impatience with the limitations of rhetorical training much more reminiscent of what we find in the *Dialogus*. In *On the Orator*, his first and most substantial work on oratory, the discussion of technical aspects of rhetoric is interlarded with dismissive comments. So, for example, when Antonius turns in book 2 to the question of how the orator sets about his task, he says of the rhetoricians:

> But, as I far as I can judge, what they [sc. Greek teachers of rhetoric] teach is absolutely ridiculous; . . . they establish five parts of eloquence, like limbs: to find what you are to say, to arrange it once found, then to decorate it with words, afterwords to memorise it, and finally to deliver and pronounce it; and this is hardly mysterious stuff.[27]

Given the dialogue format of *On the Orator*, it would be unsound to assume that Antonius is Cicero's mouthpiece; in the passage referred to above on the closure of the Latin schools, Crassus, the other main interlocutor, talks relatively positively about Greek teachers of rhetoric. But Crassus also seems to be impatient with systematic exposition; so, when he handles figures of speech, he does so very briefly (3.201–208), offering in their place little more than a list of technical names for different effects.

Others of Cicero's oratorical works deal with very specific aspects of rhetoric at a high level of detail and concept: they are not works for beginners.[28] And although Cicero is undoubtedly concerned in them to secure his lasting reputation, he is largely interested in defending his own practice as an orator – now finished, as he thought at the time of composition – rather than establishing a new reputation as an educator. Indeed, *Brutus* and *Orator* show very clear signs of being influenced by the controversy over Atticism, which I discussed in Chapter 3.

[27] Cicero, *On the Orator* 3.77–79, *sed tamen est eorum doctrina, quantam ego iudicare possum, perridicula: ... dedinde quinque faciunt quasi membra eloquentiae, inuenire quid dicas, inuenta disponere, deinde ornare uerbis, post memoriae mandare, tum ad extremum agere ac pronuntiare; rem sane non reconditam.*

[28] *On the Orator* offers a treatment of prose rhythm; *Topica* explores the application of philosophical argument to the law. See Narducci (2002); Reinhardt (2003).

These mature works of Cicero are, in short, not very useful as guides for beginners in learning how to speak well. In common with Tacitus' *Dialogus*, they are written by someone who was completely in control of the oratorical medium but not primarily concerned with transmitting skills to beginners. Rather, oratory's intimate relationship with the conduct of the Roman state and the ambitions of its elite made it a productive system of knowledge with which to explore the defects and anxieties of the political life.[29]

However, rhetorical works which do focus on the straightforwardly useful communication of knowledge have a tendency towards tedium and even unreadability for an audience which is not using them as textbooks to learn how to speak: an indication of which is the relative lack of modern studies of the great bulk of instructional works which survive from the imperial period. Quintilian's *Education of the Orator* occupies a position which we might regard as intermediate. It suggests very strongly that he was himself a great teacher; and his work sets conscientiously about the task of communicating the elements of effective oratory in a clear and systematic manner. But it is far more than simply a textbook. Quintilian's own *persona* and motivations are openly displayed; his generally critical views of contemporary oratory and rhetorical training are forcefully expressed; and there is a deep historical awareness throughout the work which is reflected most clearly in the loving accumulation of examples from great orators of the past, above all Cicero. He is concerned with the whole of the orator's education, from early childhood onwards, and in the twelfth book turns to a range of ethical and professional questions about the orator's behaviour once he has begun to practise; systematic instruction is supplemented by an awareness of what the orator does when he has finished with formal education.[30]

The various examples of Cicero, Tacitus and Quintilian demonstrate the limitations of the rhetorical handbook from the perspective of a writer wishing to explore oratory as a phenomenon. From the students' perspective, also, the information in handbooks was not enough, on its own, to create an effective orator. Practice was necessary. Aspiring orators put the skills they were learning into effect by composing, memorising and delivering short speeches on set, artificial topics. This form of exercise is described by the general name of declamation, but assessing declamation in practice is difficult because

---

[29] Winterbottom (2001); Mayer (2001); Steel (2003); Fantham (2004).
[30] Kennedy (1969); Morgan (1998b).

it was also a popular pastime among established orators. Four collections of declamatory material exist: the elder Seneca's collection, the minor and major declamations ascribed to Quintilian, and Calpurnius Flaccus' collection of declamations.[31] There seem to have been two types of declamatory exercise: the *controuersia* and the *suasoria*.[32] A *suasoria* offered a simulacrum of a deliberative debate, and often took its subject from history: whether or not Hannibal should march on Rome was an extremely hackneyed example.[33] The *controuersia* provided practice in forensic oratory: it posed a legal problem and expected responses for and against. An example from Calpurnius is, 'Some young men used regularly to go to a brothel. After the brothel keeper had often warned them not to come, he dug a pit and filled it with fire. When the young men came, they were burnt alive. The brothel keeper is accused by the parents of harming the state.'[34] The greater complexity of argumentation in *controuersiae* and the legal knowledge which they required meant that they normally followed *suasoriae* in the school curricula.

As a teaching tool, such practice exercises could clearly be extremely effective, despite the formulaic and apparently even artificial quality of the subject matter.[35] However, declamation was also a popular pastime for adults. Overwhelming evidence of this comes above all from the elder Seneca's collections of material from declamations, *Controuersiae* and *Suasoriae*. Seneca's collection is interspersed with anecdotes which give a sense of the environment in which these declamations were being created: men who were established orators declaiming for pleasure alongside teachers of rhetoric.

It would be easy, though misleading, to construct a narrative of declamation which connects its popularity with a decline in 'proper' oratory in the imperial period. The four surviving collections of declamatory material in Latin are indeed all from the first and second centuries A.D.; but it is clear that declamation existed as an exercise for adults during the late Republic.[36] And insofar as declamation did

---

[31] For a brief survey, see Sussman (1994: 5–6).

[32] Bonner (1949); Bonner (1977).

[33] Juvenal, *Satires* 7.160–164.

[34] Calpurnius 5, *iuuenes frequenter ad lupanar ueniebant. cum his leno frequenter dununtiasset ne accederent, foueam fecit et compleuit ignibus. adulescentes cum uenissent, exusti sunt. accusatur a parentibus eorum leno laesae rei publicae.*

[35] One could argue that practice legal cases need to be artificial, in order to test rules. For ancient criticism, see Sussman (1994: 14–16).

[36] See Cicero, *Letters to Friends* 7.33.

offer skills useful for the orator, the excitement it clearly generated among some in the imperial period is testament rather to the continuing importance of oratory than to a decline in interest. However, recent criticism is increasingly emphasising declamation's status as a distinct genre, whose preoccupations and themes deserve attention in themselves.[37]

Nonetheless, thinking about declamation may contribute to understanding how aspiring orators made the transition from education and practice to actual speaking. The surviving declamations demonstrate deep interest in finding arguments for both sides of cases. The elder Seneca does not, with one exception only, provide complete speeches delivered in response to topics, but analyses declamatory themes in terms of the epigrams which were included in declaimers' speeches, the analyses of the points at question, and finally the lines of argument.[38] The lines of argument are called *colores*. Revealingly, Quintilian handles *colores* in his section on false narratives; indeed, he seems to offer an etymology for the use of the term which connects it with blushing for embarrassment.[39] In book 12, at the point where he discusses the circumstances under which someone might speak for a bad cause, he imagines someone saying, 'Why have you discussed colours and the defence of difficult cases, and even confession, unless sometimes force and skill in speaking conquer the truth itself?'[40] Facility in devising arguments involved facility in devising arguments on both sides of the case, and hence, in forensic cases, for the guilty as well as the innocent. The skills inculcated and honed by declamation were not only the ability to use language effectively and to structure speech. They included, too, training in the intellectual flexibility to construct a case in support of any line of argument. And that was a vital skill for orators in the Roman courts, whose clients could not always be innocent.[41]

Romans learnt how to become orators through the experience of a range of knowledge and relationships. They were exposed to a curriculum of rhetoric borrowed from the Greeks, modified to

---

[37] Imber (2001); Gunderson (2004).

[38] The exception seems to be *Controuersia* 2.7. See Winterbottom (1974: xv–xx).

[39] Quintilian, *Education of the Orator* 4.2.88.

[40] Quintilian, *Education of the Orator* 12.1.33, *cur tu de coloribus et difficilium causarum defensione, nonnihil etiam de confessione locutus es, nisi aliquando uis ac facultas dicendi expugnat ipsam ueritatem?* Cf. *Education of the Orator* 11.1.81.

[41] On the moral dilemma of defending the guilty, see particularly Cicero, *On Duties* 2.51; Quintilian, *Education of the Orator* 12.1.33–45.

reflect Roman law and society, which was itself developing in the ever more closely integrated worlds of Greece and Rome as the imperial period progressed. They practised this rhetorical knowledge on themes derived from the wilder shores of Roman experience and then they began to exercise their abilities on real cases within a society where personal connections were essential to success and recognition.

CONCLUSION

On the front cover of this book is an image of a coin minted in 45 B.C. It shows the speaker's platform (*rostra*) in the Roman forum, decorated with the beaks of ships captured from the Antiates in 341 B.C., and the tribunes' bench. Above the image is the name of the coiner: '*PALIKANUS*'. It is an appropriate image for a book which has been concerned above all with oratory as a series of occasions which happened at specific times and places and which derived its importance from the fact of performance. However, from that perspective any image of the *rostra* would be suitable.

The *rostra* is an unusual image to have on a coin of the Republican period. Palicanus' coin was minted during Caesar's dictatorship: a period during which the normal routines and mechanisms of the Roman constitution, including popular oratory, were profoundly disturbed. On the other side of this coin, however, is a woman's head, identified by lettering on the coin as *Libertas*, freedom. This coin is thus relating popular oratory to the concept of freedom. The most obvious reference for this image is the actions of M. Lollius Palicanus, tribune of the people in 71 B.C., when he agitated for the complete restoration of tribunician rights which had been severely restricted by Sulla.[1] The moneyer, presumably his son, was thus using his office to preserve the memory of his family. But it is rather striking that this coin appears at a time when both oratory and freedom seemed, to many members of the elite, at least, to be under profound threat.

Too little is known of Palicanus and the circumstances of his coining to be sure of what he wanted his coin to mean, though it is very attractive to conclude that it is an assertion that genuine freedom has been secured through Caesar.[2] But what it does encapsulate in visual form is that oratory, and the possibilities of oratory, are one of the ways in which Romans thought about their state and its operation. The orators whose words and actions have formed the material for this book were concerned for much of their time with private concerns: their reputation in relation to their rivals, their successes and failures in the courts, their capacity to attract the support of the people or the emperor. Ultimately, however, oratory at Rome was at the heart of how those who ran the Roman state understood their

---

[1] M. Crawford (1974: 482–483).

role, their importance, and their identity. The surviving written speeches give us a literary genre containing examples of great power and skill; full understanding of why that power and skill matter is grounded in the locations of Roman oratory and in the occasions when men spoke there.

---

[2] See Weinstock (1971: 133–142) for Caesar's appeal to *libertas*.

BIBLIOGRAPHY

Adams, J. N. (2003). *Bilingualism and the Latin Language*. Cambridge, Cambridge University Press.

Albert, S. (1980). *Bellum Iustum*. Kallmünz, Lassleben.

Aldrete, G. S. (1998). *Gestures and Acclamations in Ancient Rome*. Baltimore, Johns Hopkins University Press.

Astin, A. E. (1978). *Cato the Censor*. Oxford, Oxford University Press.

Axer, J. (1979). *The Style and the Composition of Cicero's Speech 'Pro Q. Roscio Comoedo': Origin and Function*. Warsaw.

Beard, M., and Crawford, M. (1999). *Rome in the Late Republic: Problems and Interpretations*. London, Duckworth.

Benner, M. (1975). *The Emperor Says: Studies in the Rhetorical Style of the Edicts of the Early Empire*. Goteborg.

Berry, D. H. (1996). *Cicero pro Sulla Oratio*. Cambridge, Cambridge University Press.

Bonnefond-Coudry, M. (1989). *Le Sénat de la République romaine de la Guerre d'Hannibal à Auguste: pratiques délibératives et prise de décision*. Rome, École française de Rome.

Bonner, S. F. (1949). *Roman Declamation in the Late Republic and Early Empire*. Liverpool, Liverpool University Press.

—— (1977). *Education in Ancient Rome: From the Elder Cato to the Younger Pliny*. London, Methuen.

Bosworth, B. (1999). 'Augustus, the Res Gestae and Hellenistic theories of apotheosis', *Journal of Roman Studies* 89: 1–18.

Braund, S. M. (1998). 'Praise and protreptic in early imperial panegyric', in *The Propaganda of Power: The Role of Panegyric in Late Antiquity*, ed. M. Whitby. Leiden, Brill.

Brunt, P. A. (1988). *The Fall of the Roman Republic*. Oxford, Oxford University Press.

Burnand, C. J. (2000). *Roman Representations of the Orator during the Last Century of the Republic*. Oxford, DPhil thesis.

—— (2004). 'The advocate as professional: the role of the patronus in Cicero's *pro Cluentio*', in *Cicero the Advocate*, ed. J. G. F. Powell and J. Paterson. Oxford, Oxford University Press: 277–290.

Butler, S. (2002). *The Hand of Cicero*. London, Routledge.

Cairns, D. L., ed. (2005). *Body Language in the Greek and Roman Worlds*. Swansea, Classical Press of Wales.

Campbell, G. (2003). *Lucretius on Creation and Evolution*. Oxford, Oxford University Press.

Classen, C. J. (1985). *Recht, Rhetorik, Politik: Untersuchungen zu Ciceros rhetorischer Strategie*. Darmstadt, Wissenschaftliche Buchgesellschaft.

Corbeill, A. (1996). *Controlling Laughter: Political Humor in the Late Roman Republic*. Princeton, Princeton University Press.

—— (2002). 'Rhetorical education in Cicero's youth', in *Brill's Companion to Cicero: Oratory and Rhetoric*, ed. J. M. May. Leiden, Brill: 23–48.

Crawford, J. W. (1984). *Cicero: The Lost and Unpublished Orations*. Gottingen.

—— (1994). *M. Tullius Cicero, the Fragmentary Speeches: An Edition with Commentary*. Atlanta, Scholars Press.

Crawford, M. H. (1974). *Roman Republican Coinage*. London, Cambridge University Press

Crook, J. A. (1955). *Consilium Principis: Imperial Councils and Counsellors from Augustus to Diocletican*. Cambridge, Cambridge University Press.

—— (1995). *Legal Advocacy in the Roman World*. London, Duckworth.

David, J.-M. (1992). *Le patronat judiciaire au dernier siècle de la Republique romaine*. Rome, École française de Rome.

Douglas, A. E. (1968). *Cicero*. Oxford, Oxford University Press.

Drummond, A. (1995). *Law, Power, Politics: Sallust and the Execution of the Catilinarian Conspirators*. Stuttgart, Franz Steiner.

Dugan, J. (2005). *Making a New Man: Ciceronian Self-Fashioning in the Rhetorical Works*. Oxford, Oxford University Press.

Dyer, R. R. (1990). 'Rhetoric and intention in Cicero's *pro Marcello*', *Journal of Roman Studies* 80: 17–30.

Edwards, C. (1993). *The Politics of Immorality in Ancient Rome*. Cambridge, Cambridge University Press.

Epstein, D. F. (1987). *Personal Enmity in Roman Politics, 218–43 BC*. London, Croom Helm.

Fantham, E. (1996). *Roman Literary Culture: From Cicero to Apuleius*. Baltimore, Johns Hopkins University Press.

—— (2004). *The Roman World of Cicero's de Oratore*. Oxford, Oxford University Press.

Farrell, J. (2001). *Latin Language and Latin Culture*. Cambridge, Cambridge University Press.

Fleck, M. (1993). *Cicero als Historiker*. Stuttgart, Teubner.

Flower, H. (1996). *Ancestor Masks and Aristocratic Culture in Roman Culture*. Oxford, Oxford University Press.

Frier, B. W. (1985). *The Rise of the Roman Jurists: Studies in Cicero's pro Caecina*. Princeton, Princeton University Press.

Garnsey, P. (1970). *Social Status and Legal Privilege in the Roman World*. Oxford, Oxford University Press.

Geffcken, K. A. (1973). *Comedy in the pro Caelio*. Leiden, Brill.

Gleason, M. (1995). *Making Men: Sophists and Self-presentation in Ancient Rome*. Princeton, Princeton University Press.

Gotoff, H. C. (1993). *Cicero's Caesarian Speeches: A Stylistic Commentary*. Chapel Hill, University of North Carolina Press.

—— (2002). 'Cicero's Caesarian orations', in *Brill's Companion to Cicero: Rhetoric and Oratory*, ed. J. M. May. Leiden, Brill.

Gowing, A. (2000). 'Memory and silence in Cicero's *Brutus*', *Eranos* 98: 39–64.

—— (2005). *Empire and Memory: The Representation of the Roman Republic in Imperial Culture*. Cambridge, Cambridge University Press.

Graf, F. (1991). 'Gestures and conventions: the gestures of Roman actors and orators', in *A Cultural History of Gesture*, ed. J. Bremmer and H. Roodenburg. Cambridge, Polity Press.

Griffin, M. T. (1976). *Seneca: A Philosopher in Politics*. Oxford, Oxford University Press.

—— (1982). 'The Lyons tablet and Tacitean hindsight', *Classical Quarterly* 32(2): 404–418.

Gruen, E. S. (1990). *Studies in Greek Culture and Roman Policy*. Leiden.

—— (1992). *Culture and National Identity in Republican Rome*, Cornell University Press.

Gunderson, E. (2000). *Staging Masculinity: The Rhetoric of Performance in the Roman World*. Ann Arbor, University of Michigan Press.

—— (2004). *Declamation, Paternity and Roman Identity*. Cambridge, Cambridge University Press.

Habinek, T. (2005). *Ancient Rhetoric and Oratory*. Oxford, Blackwell.

Hall, L. G. F. (1998). '*Ratio* and *Romanitas* in the *Bellum Gallicum*', in *Julius Caesar as Artful Reporter*, ed. K.Welch and A. Powell. Swansea, Classical Press of Wales.

Harries, J. (2004). 'Cicero and the law', in *Cicero the Advocate*, ed. J. G. F. Powell and J. Paterson. Oxford, Oxford University Press.

Harris, W. V. (1989). *Ancient Literacy*. Cambridge, MA, Harvard University Press.

Heath, M. (2004). 'Practical advocacy in Roman Egypt', in *Oratory in Action*, ed. M. Edwards and C. Reid. Manchester, Manchester University Press: 62–82.

Henderson, J. (1998). *A Roman Life: Rutilius Gallicus on Paper and in Stone*. Exeter, University of Exeter Press.

Humbert, J. (1925). *Les plaidoyers écrits et les plaidoiries réelles de Ciceron*. Paris, Presses Universitaires de France.

Imber, M. (2001). 'Practised speech: oral and written conventions in Roman declamation', in *Speaking Volumes: Orality and Literacy in the Greek and Roman World*, ed. J. Watson. Leiden, Brill.

Johnson, J. P. (2004). 'The dilemma of Cicero's speech for Ligarius', in *Cicero the Advocate*, ed. J. G. F. Powell and J. J. Paterson. Oxford, Oxford University Press.

Kaster, R. A. (1995). *Suetonius de Grammaticis et Rhetoribus*. Oxford, Oxford University Press.

Kennedy, G. A. (1969). *Quintilian*. New York, Twayne.

Kenney, E. J. (1982). 'Books and readers in the Roman world', in *The Cambridge History of Classical Literature: The Early Republic*, ed. E. J. Kenney. Cambridge, Cambridge University Press.

Kierdorf, W. (1980). *Laudatio Funebris: Interpretationen und Untersuchungen zur Entwicklung der römischen Leichenrede*. Meisenheim am Glan, Anton Hain.

Kinsey, T. E. (1971). *M. Tulli Ciceronis pro Quinctio Oratio*. Sydney, Sydney University Press.

Konstan, D. (1997). 'Friendship and monarchy: Dio of Prusa's third oration on kingship', *Symbolae Osloenses* 72: 124–143

Krostenko, B. (2001). *Cicero, Catullus and the Language of Social Performance*. Chicago, University of Chicago Press.

Laird, A. (1999). *Powers of Expression, Expressions of Power: Speech Presentation and Latin Literature*. Oxford, Oxford University Press.

Laser, G. (1997). *Populo et scaenae serviendum est : die Bedeutung der städtischen Masse in der späten Römischen Republik*. Trier, Wissenschafliche Verlag Trier.

Leeman, A. D. (1982). 'The technique of persuasion in Cicero's *pro Murena*', in *Rhetorique et Eloquence chez Ciceron*, ed. W. Ludwig. Geneva, Entretiens Hardt.

Levene, D. S. (1997). 'God and man in the classical Latin panegyric', *Proceedings of the Cambridge Philological Society* 43: 66–103.

Lintott, A. W. (1990). 'Electoral bribery in the Roman republic', *Journal of Roman Studies* 80: 1–16.

—— (1999). *The Constitution of the Roman Republic*. Oxford, Oxford University Press.

—— (2005). 'Legal procedure in Cicero's time', in *Cicero the Advocate*, ed. J. G. F. Powell and J. Paterson. Oxford, Oxford University Press.

Mack, D. (1937). *Senatsreden und Volksreden bei Cicero*. Wurzburg, K. Triltsch.

Malcovati, E. (1976). *Oratorum Romanorum Fragmenta*. Turin, Paravia.

Marinone, N. (2004). *Cronologia Ciceroniana*. Bologna, Pàtron editore.

Marrou, H.-I. (1956). *A History of Education in Antiquity*. London, Sheed and Ward.

May, J. M. (1988). *Trials of Character: The Eloquence of Ciceronian Ethos*. Chapel Hill, University of North Carolina Press.

Mayer, R. (2001). *Tacitus: Dialogus de Oratoribus*. Cambridge, Cambridge University Press.

—— (2003). 'Pliny and *gloria dicendi*', *Arethusa* 36(2): 227–234.

Millar, F. (1977). *The Emperor in the Roman World*. London, Duckworth.

—— (1998). *The Crowd in Rome in the Late Republic*. Ann Arbor, University of Michigan Press.

Mitchell, T. N. (1979). *Cicero: The Ascending Years*. New Haven, Yale University Press.

Moles, J. (1982). 'The date and purpose of the fourth kingship oration of Dio Chrysostom', *Classical Antiquity* 2(2): 251–278

Morgan, T. (1998a). *Literate Education in the Hellenistic and Roman Worlds.* Cambridge, Cambridge University Press.

—— (1998b). 'A good man skilled in politics: Quintilian's political theory', in *Pedagogy and Power: Rhetorics of Classical Language*, ed. Y. L. Too and N. Livingstone. Cambridge, Cambridge University Press.

Morstein-Marx, R. (2004). *Mass Oratory and Political Power in the Late Roman Republic.* Cambridge, Cambridge University Press.

Mouritsen, H. (2001). *Plebs and Politics in the Late Roman Republic.* Cambridge, Cambridge University Press.

Narducci, E. (2002). '*Orator* and the definition of the ideal orator', in *Brill's Companion to Cicero: Oratory and Rhetoric*, ed. J. M. May. Leiden, Brill.

Nicholson, J. (1992). *Cicero's Return from Exile: The Orations post reditum.* New York, Peter Lang.

Nisbet, R. G. M. (1961). *Cicero: In L. Calpurnium Pisonem Oratio.* Oxford, Oxford University Press.

Paterson, J. J. (2004). 'Self-reference in Cicero's forensic speeches', in *Cicero the Advocate*, ed. J. G. F. Powell and J. J. Paterson. Oxford, Oxford University Press.

Pierini, R. (2003). 'Cicerone nell'età imperiale', in E. Narducci, *Aspetti della fortuna di Cicerone nella cultura latina.* Florence, Felice le Monnier.

Pina Polo, F. (1996). *Contra arma verbis: Der Redner vor dem Volk in der späten römischen Republik.* Stuttgart, Franz Steiner Verlag.

Powell, J. G. F., and Paterson, J. J., eds. (2004). *Cicero the Advocate.* Oxford, Oxford University Press.

Ramage, E. S. (1987). *The Nature and Purpose of Augustus' Res Gestae.* Wiesbaden, Steiner.

—— (2001). 'The bellum iustum in Caesar's *de Bello Gallico*', *American Journal of Philology* 89(1): 145–170.

Ramsay, J. T. (1980). 'The prosecution of C. Manilius in 66 B.C. and Cicero's *pro Manilio*', *Phoenix* 34: 323–336.

Rawson, E. (1971). 'Lucius Crassus and Cicero: the formation of a statesman', *Proceedings of the Cambridge Philological Society* 17: 75–88.

—— (1983). *Cicero: A Portrait.* London, Bristol Classical Press.

—— (1985). *Intellectual Life in the Late Roman Republic.* London, Duckworth.

Reinhardt, T. (2003). *Cicero's Topica.* Oxford, Oxford University Press.

Richlin, A. (1992). *The Garden of Priapus: Sexuality and Aggression in Roman Humor.* New York, Oxford University Press.

—— (1999), 'Cicero's head', in *Constructions of the Classical Body*, ed. J. I. Porter. Ann Arbor, University of Michigan Press.

Riggsby, A. M. (1999). *Crime and Community in Ciceronian Rome.* Austin, University of Texas Press.

Rivière, Y. (2002). *Les délateurs sous l'Empire Romain*. Rome, École française de Rome.

Rutledge, S. H. (1999). 'Delatores and the tradition of violence in Roman oratory', *American Journal of Philology* 120(4): 555–573.

Sherwin-White, A. N. (1966). *The Letters of Pliny: A Historical and Social Commentary*. Oxford, Oxford University Press.

Small, J. P. (1997). *Wax Tablets of the Mind: Cognitive Studies of Memory and Literacy in Classical Antiquity*. London, Routledge.

Smallwood, E. M. (1967). *Documents Illustrating the Principates of Gaius, Claudius and Nero*. Cambridge, Cambridge University Press.

Steel, C. E. W. (2001). *Cicero, Rhetoric, and Empire*. Oxford, Oxford University Press.

—— (2003). 'Cicero's Brutus: the end of oratory and the beginning of history?', *Bulletin of the Institute of Classical Studies* 46: 195–211.

—— (2005). *Reading Cicero: Genre and Performance in Late Republican Rome*. London, Duckworth.

Stroh, W. (1975). *Taxis und Taktik: die advokatische Dispositionskunst in Ciceros Gerichtsreden*. Stuttgart, Teubner.

Sussman, L. A. (1994). *The Declamations of Calpurnius Flaccus*. Leiden, Brill.

Talbert, R. J. A. (1984). *The Senate of Imperial Rome*. Princeton, Princeton University Press.

Taylor, L. R. (1949). *Party Politics in the Age of Caesar*. Berkeley, University of California Press.

—— (1950). 'The date and meaning of the Vettius affair', *Historia* 1: 45–51.

Vasaly, A. (1993). *Representations: Images of the World in Ciceronian Oratory*. Berkeley, University of California Press.

Vickers, B. (1988). *In Defence of Rhetoric*. Oxford, Oxford University Press.

Walbank, F. W. (1957). *A Historical Commentary on Polybius*, vol. I, *Commentary on Books I–VI*. Oxford, Oxford University Press.

Wallace-Hadrill, A. (1982). 'Civilis princeps: between citizen and king', *Journal of Roman Studies* 72: 32–48.

Watson, J., ed. (2001). *Speaking Volumes: Orality and Literacy in the Greek and Roman World*. Leiden, Brill.

Weinstock, S. (1971). *Divus Iulius*. Oxford, Oxford University Press.

Whitmarsh, T. (2005). *The Second Sophistic*. Oxford, Oxford University Press.

Winterbottom, M. (1974). *Seneca the Elder: Declamations*. Cambridge, Harvard University Press.

—— (2001). 'Returning to Tacitus' *Dialogus*', in *The Orator in Action and Theory in Greece and Rome*, ed. C. W. Wooten. Leiden, Brill.

—— (2002). 'Believing the *pro Marcello*', in *Vertis in Usum: Studies in Honor of Edward Courtney*, ed. J. F. Miller, C. Damon and K. S. Myers. Munich, Saur.

Wisse, J. (1995). 'Greeks, Romans, and the rise of Atticism', in *Greek Literary Theory After Aristotle: A Collection of Papers in Honour of D. M. Schenkeveld,* ed. J. G. J. Abbenes, S. R. Slings and I. Sluiter. Amsterdam, VU University Press: 65–82.

Wooten, C. W. (1983). *Cicero's Philippics and their Demosthenic Model*. Chapel Hill, University of North Carolina Press.

Yakobson, A. (1999). *Elections and Electioneering in Rome*. Stuttgart, Franz Steiner.

INDEX

acting, 54-55
advocacy, 14, 29-31, 55-56
Aelius, L. Stilo, 30 n.22
Aemilius, M. Lepidus, 9
Aemilius, L. Paullus, 32
Aemilius, M. Philemon, 9
Aemilius, M. Scaurus, 57
Aesopus, 54
Annaeus, L. Seneca, the elder, 58, 75-76
Annaeus, L. Seneca, the younger, 23, 39, 53-54
Annius, T. Milo, 60
Antiochus III, 19
Antiochus of Ascalon, 65
Antonius, M., (cos. 99), 31-32, 60, 65, 73
Antonius, M., (triumvir), 51, 59-61
appearance, 52
Apuleius, 24 n.84, 34 n.36
Asconius, Q. Pedianus, 26
asianism, 57-59
Athens, 18-19, 29, 31, 67
atticism, 57-58, 73
audiences, of oratory, 4-12, 25-26, 30, 48-50, 52-53, 57, 63
Augustus, 20, 42-43, 51
auspices, 4

Bellona, temple of, 11
Bona Dea, ceremony of, 14
bribery, 46-47, 50

Caecilius, L. Metellus (cos. 251, 247), 45
Caecilius, L. Metellus, (cos. 68), 19-20
Caecilius, Q. Metellus (cos. 205), 45
Caecilius, Q. Metellus Numidicus, 8
Caelius, M. Rufus, 55
Calpurnius, L. Bibulus, 9
Calpurnius Flaccus, 75
Calpurnius, L. Piso, 51-52
calumnia, 56 n.55
Carneades, 67-68
causa Curiana, 15
censorship, 4
Claudius, (emperor), 40-43, 55
Claudius, C. Marcellus, 22-23
Cluentius, A. Habitus, 32
Clodius, P., 8, 9
colores, 76
Comum, 35
contio, 4-11, 20, 49-50
contional oratory, 4-11
Corinth, 18

Cornelius, M. Fronto, 29
Cornelius, P. Scipio Nasica, 49 n.18
Cornelius, L. Sulla, 13, 15, 79
Cornelius, Tacitus, 36-37, 39, 64-65, 74
Critolaus, 67

declamation, 74-76
defence, 16, 56
deliberative oratory, 16-17
Demosthenes, 28, 58
Dio Chrysostom, 24
Diodotus, 65
Diogenes, 67
diplomacy, 16-20
Domitian, 40
Domitius, Cn. Ahenobarbus, 71

education, 27-28, 63-80
elections, 3, 20, 49
emperor, role of, 20-21, 38-43
epideictic oratory, 22-24, 39
equestrians, 10
Erucius, 56
exile, 7-8
extortion court, 10, 15

Fabius, Q. Pictor, 17
Fannius, C., 57 n.62
Fidenae, 21
funerals, 11, 39
    oratory at, 11-12, 22, 50-51

Gabinius, A., 51
Gaul, 40-43
gesture, 4, 53-55
Greek language, use of, 18-20, 24, 71-73

Hannibal, 75
Hermagoras, 70
Hortensius, Q. Hortalus, 6, 33, 53 n.32, 54, 58

Illyria, 17-18
invective, 50-52
Isaeus, 37

Julius, C. Caesar, 9-10, 13-14, 22-23, 34, 41, 51, 79
Junius, M. Brutus, 13-14
Junius, Dec. Silanus, 13
Jupiter Capitolinus, temple of, 12
Jupiter Stator, temple of, 13